THE IRISH

COUNTRYWOMEN'S ASSOCIATION

BOOK OF CRAFTS

THE IRISH
COUNTRYWOMEN'S
ASSOCIATION

BOOK OF CRAFTS

40 PROJECTS TO MAKE AT HOME

MERCIER PRESS
IRISH PUBLISHER - IRISH STORY

Page 2: This beautiful example of tatting is included here
in memory of Rose Harris, Sevenhouses Guild, Kilkenny, who is sadly
no longer with us.

MERCIER PRESS
Cork
www.mercierpress.ie

ISBN: 978 1 78117 234 6

10 9 8 7 6 5 4 3 2 1

A CIP record for this title is available from the British Library

Printed and bound in the EU.

Contents

Store and Keep

Celebrate

Acknowledgements

The ICA has always practised the teaching of crafts and we hold regular craft competitions and craft displays at our own meetings and at events nationwide. The idea behind *The Irish Countrywomen's Association Book of Crafts* was to share the many skills and expert knowledge that exists among our members, and it is great to see our newest book come to fruition.

I am very proud of all our members who have taken the time to make detailed submissions to this book. Each member submitted a piece of craft work, some photographs, a history and a detailed summary of how to make each craft. Unfortunately, not all of the craft work submitted has been included, but this was usually because the pieces were so intricate, requiring such an expert level of skill, that they would be beyond the scope of this book to try to teach them.

I would like to thank each and every member for their wonderful contributions. Without them this book could not have come into being. I also wish to thank Joanne Dunne for her professional handling of all submissions, Joanne Murphy and Orla Neligan for their beautiful photography in the book, and Sarah Liddy, Dominic Perrem and all the team at Mercier Press for creating this book of which I am enormously proud.

Liz Wall, National President of the ICA

Introduction

As National President of the Irish Countrywomen's Association I was very pleased to be asked to write the introduction for *The ICA Book of Crafts*. The ICA has published two books during my presidency: *The ICA Cookbook* and *The ICA Book of Home and Family*, so it seemed only natural to follow on with another book showcasing one tremendously important aspect of our history – our traditional Irish crafts. These days many of us do not have time in our lives to spend making everything we wear or use, but a revival has begun and there is a growing interest in learning some of what we in the ICA call our 'heritage' crafts, as well as some more modern crafts, including upcycling and decoupage. But first, let me start with a short introduction to the ICA itself.

The ICA has made a difference, a profound, measurable and marvellous difference, to the way generations of Irish women live their lives. The ICA was central to the setting up of the co-operative movement, the credit union movement, breast health initiatives and Montessori pre-school education and has been an advocate on a huge variety of issues. The members of this organisation have made an exceptional contribution to enriching the lives of the communities in which they live and advancing the role of Irish women in society as a whole. Since the founding of our association, originally called the Society of United Irishwomen, Irish society has changed dramatically and for the better for Irish women.

The ICA's purpose has always been the betterment of women and it has worked to empower women through education and through addressing specific grievances during its existence. Although cloaked in tradition, women have used our association to improve their own lives and the lives of their families and communities.

The ICA has been a strong vehicle for change over the past hundred years. We have been a meeting ground for women from the big house to the cottage, from the Catholic and Protestant religions, from wealthy landowners to poorer immigrants. We are firm believers in self-help and community co-operation. We are non-religious, non-sectarian and non-party political, and this has contributed in a large part to our success, as we give a voice to all women.

The idea behind the organisation arose from the AGM of the Irish Agricultural Asso-ciation in December 1909, which George Russell addressed, saying: 'Every Irish community should make its own ideals and should work for them. We cannot build up a rural civilisation in Ireland without the aid of Irish women.' This passionate plea made a profound impression on the women attending that AGM and they came out of that meeting determined to embark on organising a new association. On 8 May 1910 a meeting was called in Anita Lett's home to organise a women's rural organisation. In her opening paper, entitled 'The Scheme Explained', she argued that Irishwomen, regardless of class and creed, could unite for the common good of the country. The scheme covered many areas of life including the deficiency of good-quality nursing and health care, adequate nutrition for children, education, horticulture and dress. The scheme also outlined how the new organisation was to be governed. Branches were to be set up in every parish. These branches would be affiliated to a county organisation and an all-Ireland branch would be set up in Dublin. Local women would enjoy a good degree of autonomy in their local branch and the end of the scheme shows Anita Lett urging them to unite and achieve their goals. The fact that we still meet in autonomous Guilds, have Federation or County committees and unite to achieve our goals shows how solid the foundations laid down all those years ago were.

The main objective of the ICA when it was first founded as the United Irishwomen in 1910 was to bring women together in fellowship and friendship and to develop and improve their wellbeing, knowledge and skills, as well as improving the general quality of life in Ireland through the co-operative effort of women. Even the fact that it began meeting without men, to discuss women's needs and to improve their education and skills, was a very radical action for that era.

Another of the organisation's early agendas was to work together to achieve better living conditions for all, as can be seen in this quote from a 1910 paper:

> It is essential to Ireland that her rural population should be strong, healthy and active. It must remain on the land, happily occupied, well employed, socially and intellectually developed. Here is permanent work for women to do and UI is the organisation best qualified to help them. We had no special training for doing what we intended to do and we, none of us, aspired to reform society or preach any gospel but that of domestic economy, good comradeship and truth.

The first detailed minute book of the association, covering the years from its foundation up to 1921, gives a fascinating insight into the formative decade of the United Irishwomen. Between December 1910 and December 1911, seventeen branches were set up. There were also individual subscriptions from sixty-four married women, nine titled women, eighty-one unmarried women and two French women. Twenty-four gardens were started, and sewing classes, cookery classes and Irish classes were all set up. Up to this time craft work would have been taught at home, with many families specialising in one particular craft, safeguarding traditional methods and family secrets for generations – now they had a chance to pass these on to others.

The same minute book shows how important it was for members to be kept up to date with the latest information and there is a subscription to *Irish Homestead* and *Bean na hÉireann* (the newspaper of Inghinidhe na hÉireann), as well as a subscription for library services entitling them to borrow thirty books at a time. The ICA's founders believed that education would add to social and economic reform in the country as a whole.

In May 1912 the United Irishwomen launched their own publication, also entitled *The United Irishwomen*, and it was *the* journal for Irish countrywomen. By 1914 the title had been changed to *The Irishwoman*.

In the following decade, in 1927, Lucy Franks took a stall at the RDS Spring Show to sell handcrafts and the produce and baskets produced by the branches. The stall made a profit of £50, which led to the setting-up of a school of basket-making in Wexford. By 1929 profits from the RDS spring show had risen to £95 and the following year £102 was made. The UI set about organising courses of instruction in simple crafts for new branches and provided an income for them to invite lecturers. This did much to revive traditional crafts and brought new hope and life to these crafts in Ireland.

Two other milestones in the history of the United Irishwomen occurred in the late 1920s. The first of these was the holding of the first UI summer school. In the summer of 1929 Olivia Hughes of Fethard, Co. Tipperary, invited craft teachers from all over Ireland to join her on the slopes of Slievenamon (which translates as The Mountain of the Women) to exchange ideas and skills and to study poetry, drama and singing. The summer school that the modern Irish summer knows so well was born. All the women camped on the mountainside, which was considered a rather mad idea at the time. They learned how to make baskets in rush and cane, how to seat chairs with cane seating and how to work with leather, and enjoyed lectures in Irish poetry and local geology. Local farmers provided contributions of eggs, soda bread and cakes. From that informal gathering on the side of that lovely mountain has grown the annual summer school and it culminated in the gift of An Grianán by the Kellogg Foundation, Ireland's first residential adult education college.

Numbers grew steadily from 1929, and by the mid-1930s two summer schools were run each year and each Guild was limited to one delegate per year, although an effort was made to fit in delegates from newly formed Guilds. Even the war years, when transport had virtually come to a standstill, did not deter the summer schools.

No longer held on a mountainside, the summer schools now took place in an empty house owned by Dr O'Connell in Tipperary, father of two stalwart members. The staffing of the schools was voluntary and the work of the house was divided into shifts and duties allocated amongst the groups. The mornings were devoted to classes which included such diverse subjects as the Irish language, arithmetic, needlework, embroidery, dressmaking, knitting, basket making, house decoration, spinning, dyeing, weaving, rug making, sheepskin curing, glove making, carpentry, cooking, laundry, colour and design. All the delegates attended health talks and were involved in keep-fit exercises and games. The afternoons were left free for expeditions and the evenings were devoted to music and singing, dancing, drama, verse-speaking, lectures, debates and discussions. Members attending the summer schools were expected to learn all that they possibly could and to take that knowledge back to their Guild. The association received no funding to run these summer schools, so many Department of Education teachers gave the courses during their free time for no payment.

The summer schools were held every summer from 1929 to 1953 in different parts of the country, until the opening of An Grianán in 1954.

The second milestone was the formation of the Country Workers. The United Irish-women had made great inroads into educating the women of Ireland and at the end of the 1920s turned their attention to enabling women to make their own money by selling their homemade produce. This was singularly the most important aspect of helping isolated craft workers in rural areas to improve their production of home-made crafts and to support them in home industries. For many women, making and producing high quality crafts was the only source of income for themselves. The result was the opening of the Country Shop on St Stephen's Green (with a restaurant to finance it) and the formation of the Country Workers Ltd, which was a not-for-profit company, to direct the activities. The Country Workers Ltd had two stated objectives:

- To help people in small farm areas in the West of Ireland by encouraging and supporting home industries such as handspinning, weaving and knitting.

- To encourage craftworkers throughout the country and to promote country crafts and country produce generally, with special emphasis on developing co-operative working practices.

The three directors were Lucy Franks, Olivia Hughes and Muriel Gahan. Together these three women were an outstanding force to be reckoned with. The country shop opened in 1930 and closed its doors for the last time in 1978. It became the centre for traditional crafts and a haven for rural people visiting Dublin. The Country Shop was an excellent opportunity to showcase and promote some of the excellent talent in rural Ireland. Exhibitions were regularly held there of tweeds from Kerry, patchwork quilts from Wexford, rushwork from Louth and produce from all over Ireland. There were also some more unusual exhibitions, including one in 1933 of a group of country cures. That exhibition was a collection of the traditional cures used by a Mayo woman all her life and also widely used throughout rural Ireland.

Following the success of the Country Shop, the Irish Homespun Society was set up in 1935 with ICA member Muriel Gahan as the chairperson. The Irish Homespun Society worked closely with the Irish Folklore Commission until 1959.

The ICA has always been aware of the importance of developing the social side of women's lives and the policy of the ICA over the years has been to teach country-women to tackle their own problems in a self-reliant way without depending too much on outside help. When a member learned a new skill she was expected to pass this on to other Guild members. If a member attended a conference they had to submit a report of their findings for circulation so that all members could learn through them. Classes in public speaking, running meetings, the improvement of homes and how to make handcraft for profit were all taught to members to help them become more self-reliant.

The activities of the ICA were greatly enhanced by the opening of our very own sunny place, An Grianán, in 1954. An Grianán, in Termonfeckin, Co. Louth, was gifted to the ICA by the Kellogg Foundation of America and from its inception offered a varied and wide programme of courses including arts, crafts, home advisory services, community development, community enterprise and leadership. This beautiful building, in a very picturesque setting, continues to provide courses and the opportunity to learn a craft, perfect a skill, make music and meet friends up to this present day. Classes are still taught in a wide variety of crafts, including bobbin lace work, crochet, macramé, millinery, willow work and Mountmellick embroidery.

In this new book we aim to showcase the best of the crafts that are still taught and used by ICA members today. As the submissions came into our central office, I was inspired by how many of our members are highly skilled in numerous crafts and how these crafts are still being taught in our Guilds around the country. Every year the ICA holds Handcraft Week in An Grianán, when all the ICA craft teachers get together and teach their own crafts to each other and to other ICA members, augmenting their own skills and learning something new as well. All the teachers hold an ICA craft teacher's award and delight in passing on their skills and their learning. Every year Handcraft Week sells out and bookings are taken on the last day for the following year as it is so popular and is also an excellent opportunity for networking. Some great parties are held in the evenings too!

I have really enjoyed seeing all the different types of crafts that have been submitted and although only forty pieces have been included here they represent twenty-five crafts which are alive and well in the ICA and are being taught and learned around the country. While I am sure that some of you who will be reading this book will already know a lot about crafts and be familiar with some of the skills involved, I hope that you will enjoy learning some new skills and will help to keep these skills alive in Ireland for the benefit of future generations.

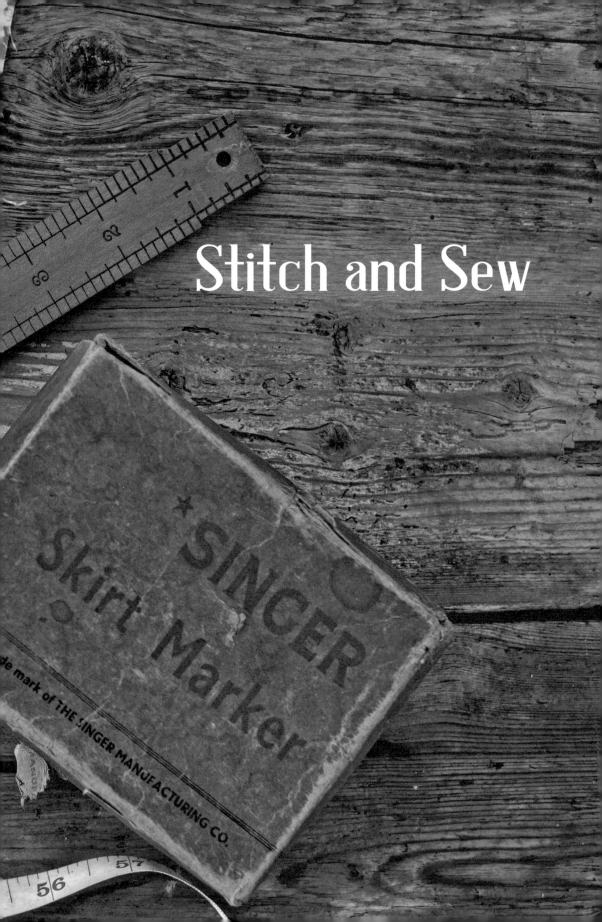

Stitch and Sew

Hairpin Crochet Stole

Nora Keady, Moycullen Guild, Galway

Hairpin crochet or hairpin lace is made using a basic loom, which consists of two thin metal rods held at the top and bottom by removable bars. Strips of lace are formed by wrapping yarn around the prongs of the loom to form loops that are held together by a row of crochet stitches worked in the centre, called the vein. This project consists of 12 strips of hairpin crochet. The strips are made individually and are joined together using a cable plait joining. The finished stole is 58cm wide and 140cm long.

You will need

Hairpin lace loom

5mm crochet hook

400g weight Aran acrylic/ wool mixture thread/yarn

Scissors

Abbreviations

ch = chain

dc = double crochet

MAKE THE STRIPS:

Use the full width of the loom for this project (10cm).

Make a slip-knot, half the width of the loom, and set up the first loop on the left side of the loom (see figure 1).

Bring the thread across the front of the loom, round to the back (see figure 2) and, holding the thread in your left hand, make a chain stitch into the loop on the left-hand side of the centre knot (see figure 3).

Push the crochet needle to the back, through the loom. Holding the needle with your right hand, the thread in your left, turn the loom towards you from right to left, wrapping the thread round the left-hand side of the loom as you turn, to make the next loop. Make a double crochet into this loop on the left-hand side of the centre vein of the strip (see figure 4).

Repeat from * to * (see figure 5) until you have 198 loops on each side of the loom. Finish by pulling the thread through the last stitch at the centre. Leave a tail of about 10cm as this will be used later when joining strips.

Tip: Place a marker after every 50 loops on each side of the strip, to save having to count several times!

Remove the strip from the loom and make another 11 strips the same, then join as detailed below.

CABLE JOIN

This join is especially suitable for thicker yarns. It gives a lovely bold texture and is suitable for stoles, throws, scarves, etc. There is no extra thread/yarn needed to make this joining. Keep all the 'twists' on the loops in the same direction.

NB: When joining successive strips, you need to alternate the order of picking up the first 3 loops of each strip, so that the fabric will be even.

Place 2 strips together, insert the crochet needle into the first 3 loops of the first strip, then into the first 3 loops of the 2nd strip, draw 3 loops of the 2nd strip through the 3 loops on needle; *draw the next 3 loops of the 1st strip through the loops on the needle, then draw the next 3 loops of the 2nd strip through the loops on the needle*. Repeat from * to * to the end of the strip. Finish by pulling the tail from the centre of the strip through the last 3 loops on the crochet needle to make another loop and finish off by pulling the end of the thread through the last loop.

Join the remainder of the strips to the first 2 in the same way, not forgetting to alternate the side when picking up the first 3 loops at the beginning of each strip.

EDGING

No extra yarn is needed for the long sides. Keep the 'twists' in the loops in the same direction.

Insert the crochet needle into the first 3 loops, then draw the next 3 loops through the loops on the needle; *insert the needle into the next 3 loops and pull through the 3 loops on the needle.* Repeat from * to * to the last 3 loops, then pull the tail from the centre of the strip through these 3 loops, make another loop and finish off. Repeat for the 2nd side of the stole.

FINISHING SHORT ENDS AND TASSELS

Join thread/yarn to the right-hand edge of the stole.

Ch 4, 1 dc into the centre vein of the first strip; ch 4, 1 dc into the centre of the joining of the first 2 strips; *ch 4, 1 dc into the centre vein of the next strip; ch 4, 1 dc into the centre of the joining of the next 2 strips*. Repeat from * to * to end.

Repeat for the second short side.

Weave in all loose threads through the centre vein of the strips.

For the tassels, cut 4 pieces of thread/yarn, each 30cm long for each of the 24 (4 ch) loops on each end of the stole. Fold each group of 4 pieces in half and pull through the loops to make tassels.

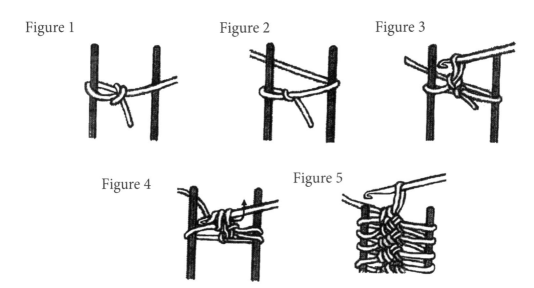

Figure 1

Figure 2

Figure 3

Figure 4

Figure 5

Crochet Cushion Cover

Breda Baker, Annascaul Guild, Kerry

Once you've mastered the basic crochet stitches, you'll be amazed how quickly you can produce beautiful projects. For instance, add texture to a room with this fabulous cushion cover. If you want to create a pop of colour choose brightly coloured crochet yarn. The cover is made up of four panels on each side and finished with a border.

You will need

8 x 50g balls of no. 20 crochet cotton

1mm crochet hook

6 poppers

Abbreviations

ch = chain

dc = double crochet

dtr = double treble

gr = group

ss = slip stitch

sp(s) = space(s)

st(s) = stitch(es)

tr = treble

yrh = yarn round hook

FOR EACH MOTIF PANEL

Make 8 ch, ss into first ch to form a ring.

1st round: 11 ch, (1 dtr into ring, 7 ch) 7 times, ss into 4th of 11 ch (8 sps).

2nd round: 1 ch, (7 dc into next 7 ch sp) 8 times.

3rd round: ss over first 3 dc of first 7 dc, 1 dc into next dc, 8 ch, (1 dc into centre dc of next 7 dc, 8 ch) 7 times, ss to first dc.

4th round: 3 ch, 9 tr into next 8 ch sp, (1 tr into next dc, 9 tr into next 8 ch sp) 7 times, ss to top of 3 ch.

5th round: (6 ch, skip 4 tr, 1 dc into next tr) 16 times.

6th round: 1 ch, (7 dc into 6 ch sp) 16 times.

7th round: as 3rd round, but repeat bracket 15 times instead of 7.

8th round: 1 ch, (9 dc into next 8 ch sp, 1 dc into next dc) 16 times.

9th round: *8 ch, skip 4 dc, 3 dtr all into next dc, leaving last loop of each dtr on hook, yrh pull through 4 loops, dtr gr formed, 8 ch, skip 4 dc, 1 dc into next dc,* repeat from * to * 15 times.

10th round: ss over next 8 ch, (1 dc into top of next dtr gr, 9 ch) 16 times, ss to first dc.

11th round: 4 ch, skip 1 st (count each ch and each dc as a st), *1 tr into next st, 1 ch, skip 1 st*, repeat from * to * all round, ss into third of 4 ch.

12th round: 8 ch, skip 3 sts, (1 dc into next st, 5 ch, skip 3 sts) 5 times, *1 tr into each of next 17 sts, 5 ch, skip 3 sts, (1 dc into next st, 5 ch, skip 3 sts) 5 times*, repeat from * to * twice more, 1 tr into each of next 16 sts, ss into 3rd of 8 ch.

13th round: ss into first 5 ch sp, 3 ch, 3 tr into same sp, *(5 ch, 4 dtr into next 5 ch sp) 4 times, 5 ch, 4 tr into next 5 ch sp, 1 tr into each of next 17 tr, 4 tr into next 5 ch sp*, repeat from * to * 3 more times, omitting last 4 tr, ss into top of 3 ch.

14th round: ss into first 5 ch sp, 3 ch, 3 tr into same sp, *(5 ch, 4 dtr into next 5 ch sp) 3 times, 5 ch, 4 tr into next 5 ch sp, 1 tr into each of next 25 tr, 4 tr into next 5 ch sp*, repeat from * to * 3 more times, omitting last 4 tr, ss into top of 3 ch.

15th round: ss into first 5 ch sp, 3 ch, 3 tr into same sp, *(5 ch, 4 dtr into next 5 ch sp) twice, 5 ch, 4 tr into next 5 ch sp, 1 tr into each of next 33 tr, 4 tr into next 5 ch sp*, repeat from * to * 3 more times, omitting last 4 tr, ss into top of 3 ch.

16th round: ss into first 5 ch sp, 3 ch, 3 tr into same sp, *5 ch, 3 dtr into next 5 ch sp, 5 ch, 4 tr into next 5 ch sp, 1 tr into each of next 41 tr, 4 tr into next 5 ch sp*, repeat from * to * 3 more times, omitting last 4 tr, ss into top of 3 ch.

17th round: ss into first 5 ch sp, 3 ch, 3 tr into same sp, *5 ch,

1 dtr into centre dtr of 3 dtr, 5 ch, 4 tr into next 5 ch sp, 1 tr into each of next 49 tr, 4 tr into next 5 ch sp*, repeat from * to * 3 more times, omitting last 4 tr, ss into top of 3 ch.

18th round: ss into first 5 ch sp, 3 ch, 3 tr into same sp, *2 tr into 1 dtr, 4 tr into next 5 ch sp, 1 tr into each of next 57 tr, 4 tr into next 5 ch sp*, repeat from * to * 3 more times, omitting last 4 tr, ss into top of 3 ch.

19th round: Work 1 dc into each tr all round, working 4 ch at each corner. Fasten off.

ASSEMBLY AND EDGING

Make 8 motifs in all and join in 2 sets of 4 for each side of the cushion. Sew together round 3 sides.

The border is worked around the 3 sewn sides of the cushion, and then on both sides of the opening. Join the thread at the corner beside the opening with a slip stitch.

1st round: 5 ch, 4 tr into same st, 4 ch, *skip 3 sts, 5 tr, 4 ch, repeat from * around the 3 sides to end, turn.

2nd round: 5 ch, 1 tr into 4 ch sp, 3 ch, ss into third st from hook. When this first picot is made, repeat into each 4 ch sp around the 3 sides.

Work these 2 rows along both sides of the opening as well. Sew on 6 small poppers for easy access, and insert a cushion pad.

Enjoy!

Allsorts Patchwork Quilt

Bridgid Keane, Ardmore Grange Guild, Waterford

Patchwork was originally a frugal way of using up scraps of fabric to create something from nothing, but nowadays packs of precut fabric in complementary patterns and colours are available, creatively named according to the shape and size of the pieces included. There are many books and Internet sites that will show you the basic techniques for piecing, quilting and binding. I had great fun mixing and matching the colours for this quilt, but it can also be made from scraps. These instructions are for a single bed quilt, measuring 170 x 235cm. Using appropriate colours, it would make a lovely baby quilt if you reduce the number of squares used to produce a quilt approximately 95 x 125cm.

You will need

1 jelly roll
(40 assorted strips 7 x 112cm)

1 charm pack
(40 assorted 13cm squares)

Contrasting or toning fabric for framing and binding

Wadding and backing fabric

Good scissors

Sewing machine
(or needle and thread if you have a lot of patience!)

Divide the squares and jelly roll strips into 3 or 4 random bundles.

Take 1 square and 1 toning or contrasting strip and cut the strip into appropriate lengths to frame the square.

Using a ½cm seam join the strip to the square. Surround the square as if for the first stage in a 'log cabin' block pattern (see figure 1) or you can do top and bottom and then both sides. This results in a 25cm square.

Continue until you have used 40 charm squares and 40 jelly roll strips.

You now have 40 x 25cm squares.

Set them out 5 squares across and 8 squares down in a way that you like, then sew them together again using a ½cm seam.

You now have a quilt panel that measures 121 x 193cm.

Sew the remaining fabric together randomly with some of the contrasting fabric to create a frame for your panel.

Take your completed quilt top, the wadding and backing fabric and quilt either by hand or machine.

Finally, use the remaining backing fabric to bind the edges of the quilt and enjoy for evermore.

Figure 1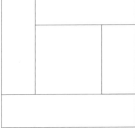

Chicken Scratching Embroidery Tea Cosy

Margaret Clince, Garristown Guild, Dublin

This is a very simple form of embroidery. It is sometimes known as Tenerife embroidery, named after needlemade Tenerife lace because of its lace-like appearance. It is worked on gingham, which usually comes in 4 count (4 squares to the inch), 8 count and 16 count. Panels of chicken scratching could be framed, used in a cushion cover or throw, incorporated into a little girl's dress or, as in these instructions, on a tea cosy. The possibilities are limited only by your imagination!

You will need

2 pieces of gingham fabric 36 x 30cm

2 pieces of pre-quilted fabric 34 x 24cm

6 strand embroidery thread in white and a colour to match the fabric (usually 2 strands are used for 4 and 8 count gingham and 1 strand for 16 count)

Embroidery needle

Sewing machine or needle and thread for assembly

You can check the Internet for pattern ideas and once you've got the hang of it you can make up your own. Work your pattern on both pieces of gingham.

There are just 3 stitches used:

The first stitch used is a double cross stitch worked by forming an X and then working a + over the top of the X. The outline is worked using this stitch on the white squares using the coloured thread. The same stitch is used worked in white on the dark squares to fill in the shapes. Just be sure that all of the top stitches in the double cross are worked in the same direction.

The second stitch is a simple straight running stitch that is worked in white over the medium shaded squares of the gingham, both horizontally and vertically.

The third stitch is a circle that is worked around the white squares by simply running the thread under the end of each surrounding straight stitch (but not through the material), twice around the square.

Work the stitches in the following order:

Do all double cross stitches on the white squares using coloured thread.

Do all double cross stitches on the dark squares using white thread.

Do all straight stitches on the medium squares using white thread.

Do all circles using white thread around the white squares.

ASSEMBLY

Once you have embroidered your pattern on the gingham, with right sides facing, stitch the two pieces of embroidered gingham together leaving the bottom side unstitched. Do the same with the two pieces of pre-quilted fabric.

Turn the gingham right side out and insert the pre-quilted fabric inside the gingham, then turn in a hem on the gingham at the bottom and hand stitch to the padding.

Smocking

Pauline O'Dwyer, Marlay Guild, Dublin

The smocked design in the dress pictured can be used as an insert in dresses, cushion covers, bags, even ornaments. Detailed instructions for the specific smocking stitches can be found easily online.

You will need

Smocking dots
(iron-on transfers which make it easy to position evenly spaced tacking stitches)

DMC embroidery threads

Cotton threads for gathering the dots

Fabric
(cotton is best; you can also use cotton gingham)

Embroidery needles

Thimble

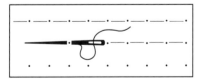

Figure 1

First of all determine the finished width of your project bearing in mind that fine fabric takes 3 to 4 times the final width and heavier fabric takes 2½ times the finished width. Also add seam allowances on all sides if your finished smoking piece is to be inserted.

You can use smocking dots or if you are lucky enough to possess a smocking pleater, by all means use it. Place the smocking dots on the wrong side of the fabric and press with a hot iron.

Next, tack along a row of dots ensuring you have one stitch at each dot with one long thread (see figure 1); leave it loose at the end of the row and continue to tack along the dots on each row until you have the length you require. Then pull the threads gently until the fabric is gathered into the size of the finished piece you wish to make and tie the ends of each 2 rows of tacking with a knot. Do not gather it too tightly so it will be easy to get the needle in and out for smocking.

There are a variety of stitches that you can choose for your smocking. It's best to start with an outline stitch for stability. You may use a knot starting

from the back and working from left to right. Below are diagrams of some common smocking stitches.

When the design is completed and before the tacking threads are removed, press the work as follows: place the smocking right side down on the ironing board. Lay a damp cloth over the wrong side and press very lightly with a hot iron. The steam heat will set the pleats.

It can be beneficial to leave the tacking threads at the top and bottom in situ until you have inserted your smocking into your finished project.

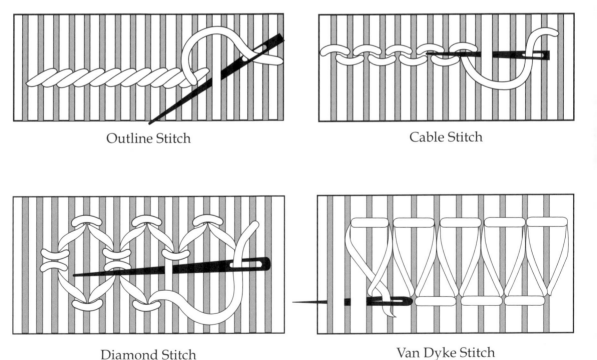

Outline Stitch

Cable Stitch

Diamond Stitch

Van Dyke Stitch

Shadow Embroidery

Carol Lynch, Muff Guild, Donegal

This is a kind of embroidery where the bulk of the stitches are on the back of the design. The embroidery thread showing through from the wrong side of the sheer fabric gives a delicate shading effect. We have photographed this project from the back to show the detail of the stitches. In order to show through nicely, use strong colours.

You will need

Sheer fabric
(organza or similar)

Fine embroidery needle
(with long eye)

Embroidery thread
(I used 2 strands and it
worked well, but you can use
3 strands)

Design

Transfer pencil

Embroidery hoop

Scissors

Thimble

Stitches used: I work shadow embroidery from the front, using closed herringbone stitch. Stem stitch, satin stitch and French knots were also used in this project. Instructions for these stitches can be found in any good embroidery book.

Apply your design to the sheer fabric using a suitable transfer pencil and a light box or, as I do, tape it to the window and trace it.

Work your design using any suitable embroidery stitches. I always leave a long tail when starting, instead of a knot or double stitches, then weave the tail in on the wrong side. I end in the same manner, giving a neater finish.

To complete your item machine or hand stitch a hem. Remove transfer pencil marks following manufacturer's instructions or soak in cold water. Do not iron or starch before washing for the first time. Do not use washing powder containing bleach. Don't wring out – hang on the line to drip, then press using a very cool iron.

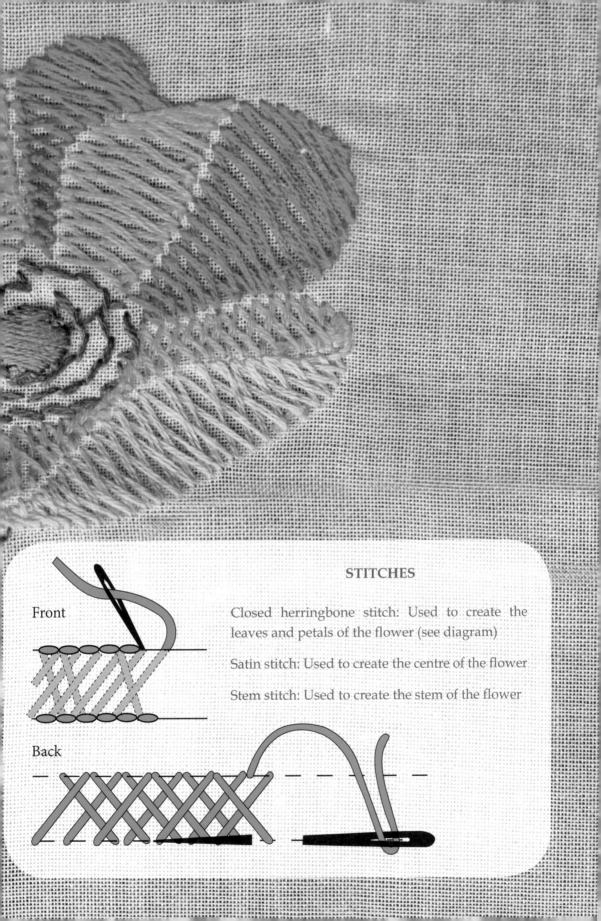

Front

Back

STITCHES

Closed herringbone stitch: Used to create the leaves and petals of the flower (see diagram)

Satin stitch: Used to create the centre of the flower

Stem stitch: Used to create the stem of the flower

Redwork Embroidery Cushion Cover

Mairead Cullen O'Gorman, Camross Guild, Wexford

Redwork embroidery is becoming very popular again and rightly so. If you like an easy and relaxing type of embroidery, this is for you. With good white cotton fabric, red embroidery floss and two or three basic embroidery stitches, you can make beautiful cushions, framed pictures, tablecloths, doilies and bed linen, or you can add a little design to the corners of handkerchiefs. One never has to think too hard about colour – it's only red!

You will need

1m good quality 100% white cotton fabric or unbleached muslin

25cm red fabric for borders and sashings

Quilting or embroidery needle

1 skein 6-strand embroidery floss

Embroidery hoop (optional but recommended)

Markers – an H2 pencil or a washable fabric-marking pen.

DESIGN

I have provided a floral design here, but there are many designs available to buy, or you can draw your own – just remember to keep it simple.

PREPARING MATERIALS

The red fabric must be washed in hot water, to make sure that it is colourfast and doesn't shrink. When dry, press the fabric. Should the fabric shrink or run a lot, discard it.

I like to use DMC 321 dark red floss. Anchor floss is also excellent to use. Both of these are colourfast.

For best results use an embroidery hoop for your project. The hoop holds the fabric taut while stitching. There are several types on the market but the plastic hoop with screw on top is the best. If you can get a hoop that covers all of the design within it, that is an added bonus.

STITCHES

Stem stitch is the most popular stitch to use. One can also use back stitch. Other stitches are French knots and satin stitch. The French knot is used for dots or eyes. Craft shops sell little embroidery stitch books – they are like gold dust to an embroiderer.

GETTING
STARTED

Cut the white or off-white fabric a little larger than the size of the project to be worked on – this allows for better room in the hoop. Too much pulling and tugging of the fabric in the hoop knocks the square out of kilter. Centre the fabric over the design pattern and trace. If using a pencil don't press too hard – use a light hand. If using a fabric marker follow the manufacturer's directions for proper use. No tracing lines should be seen on the finished work. Use a light box or window to trace patterns. When you are pleased with your tracing, then you can put your embroidery fabric into the hoop.

Before you start to embroider, wash your hands – this helps to avoid soiling. Separate the embroidery floss into two or three strands. Two strands are usual. Thread your needle and put a tiny knot at the end of your floss. Cut off the tail behind the knot. Bring your needle up from the back of the design and start to work the stem stitch.

THE PROJECT

Work slowly at first. To finish off push the needle to the back and weave the needle through the last few stitches and cut off. Never carry the red floss across to an unworked area. It would show through on the finished project. Should you feel unsure of your stitches, do a little practice piece. Once you have a rhythm going you can start your main design.

FINISHING

When all the embroidery is complete, remove the project from the hoop and wash in warm water. Rinse twice and lay out flat to dry. To press, place embroidery face down on a towel on an ironing board. Press well. The towel prevents the stitches from flattening on the fabric.

To edge the cushion cover, cut a 4cm width of red fabric to sew to the right and left side, then the top and bottom. Press seam allowances to the darker fabric.

Attach the back of the cushion to the top by sewing around three sides. Insert a pillow form, a little larger than the cushion cover, and stitch the opening closed.

Floral Template

Cross-stitch Bookmark

Pat O'Looney, Botanic Glasnevin Guild, Dublin

A personalised bookmark makes a lovely present. Choose the appropriate initial from the chart on the next page.

You will need

30 x 15cm piece of Aida fabric, 11 gauge

Embroidery cotton in the following colours:

Yellow (Anchor 289)

Green (Anchor 266)

Red (Anchor 347)

Blue (Anchor 122)

Navy (Anchor 150)

Crewel tapestry needle

Piece of white felt, 7.5 x 28cm

PVA glue

Using a tacking stitch and light coloured thread, mark the centre of the Aida across the width and down the length. The finished bookmark will be 33 squares wide by 123 squares long.

Following figure 1 do the outline border in blue thread using 2 strands of embroidery thread throughout.

Work the heart in red thread. Make sure to finish off your work neatly, as any stray threads will show through when you are finished and spoil your work.

Work the blue flower and leaves. Using the navy thread, backstitch around the flower and put 4 straight stitches from the outside to the centre of the flower.

Work the small yellow flowers. Put 4 straight stitches in blue going towards the centre of each flower.

Using your chosen letter from the alphabet (see figure 2), count across the widest part of the letter and pencil in the centre line on the chart. Your central line for stitching your design is already marked on the aida with the tacking thread.

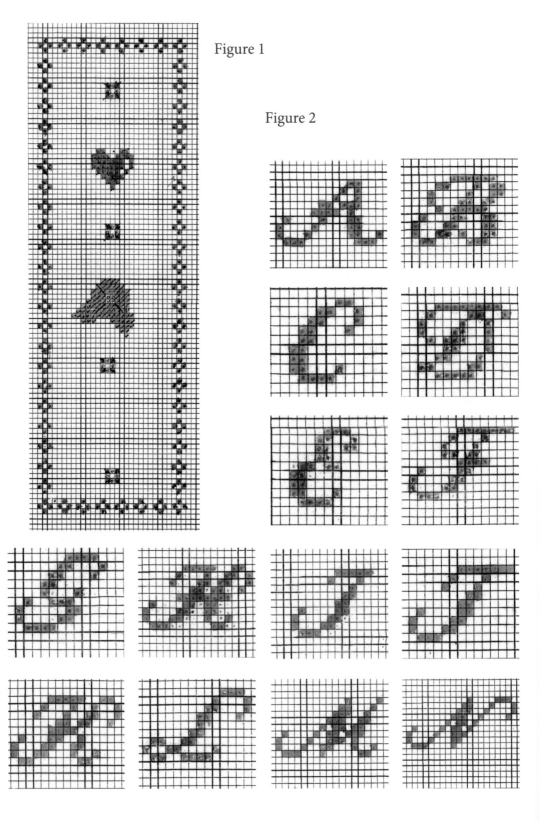

Figure 1

Figure 2

Stitch the letter in navy and outline it in backstitch in navy.

Fold excess fabric down the length to the back of the work and press the bookmark. If the Aida overlaps at the back you may trim it so that the two raw edges meet in the middle. Use an odd spot of PVA glue to keep this excess fabric in place (but use sparingly as you don't want it to seep through to the front of the work).

Fray the top and bottom of the bookmark leaving about 8 rows unfrayed between the border and the fringe.

Trim the felt to about 3mm smaller than the overall size of the bookmark. Put a very light coating of PVA on the felt and place it down on the back of the bookmark. Use the flat of your hand to press it in place.

Figure 2 continued

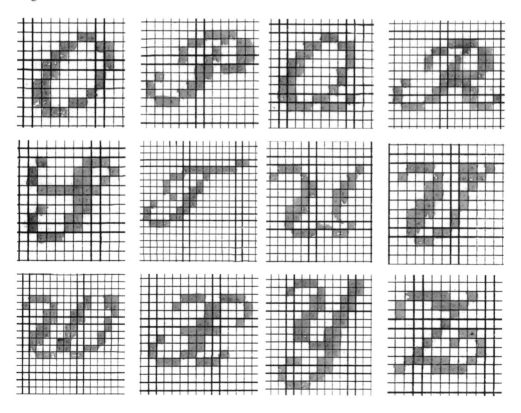

Rag Rug

Anne Payne, Portlaoise Guild, Laois

A rag rugger is an inexpensive tool, a bit like narrow, pointed spring-loaded pliers, that grips the pieces of fabric to pull them through the base material. This really is simple to do and provides a great result for little outlay. I completed the project photographed simply using an old sheet, but instructions here are for a more colourful squared pattern. You can use any design you like.

You will need

A rectangle of hessian 58 x 43cm (or however big you want your rug to be)

Fabric marker

Cutting gauge
(optional but very helpful)

Rag rugger

Material to use for the rags – any kind will do but not material that will ravel and the thicker the rags the better

Strong thread

Sharp scissors

Leaving 5cm for a hem around the edge of the fabric, use a fabric marker to draw a 5cm border on the right side of the hessian. Then divide the rectangle into 4 rows of three 12cm squares if you want to make squares of different coloured rags, otherwise a line round the outside will be enough.

Tear or cut the material for the rags into strips about 9cm long x 2.5cm wide. You don't need to cut each one individually: if you have a cutting gauge then wrap a length of rag around the gauge like a bandage, holding the groove upwards. Slip the blade of a pair of scissors into the groove and cut through the rag – all the pieces will be the correct length.

It is best to start at the edge of a square. Push the rag rugger under 2 or 3 strands of hessian as far as it will go. Squeeze the handles to open the jaws, grab one end of a rag strip and release the top handle. Then pull the rag halfway through and release it from the rag rugger. There is no need to knot the rags as the amount of rags will keep them together. Continue applying rags leaving 4 or 5 strands of hessian between each rag. You can use a different colour in each square and then one colour for the whole border area. Continue until the rag rug is the required size or all the squares are filled.

Press the hem to the wrong side of the rug, folding it neatly at each corner, and sew down using the strong thread. Turn your rug over and ruffle the rags to even out the pile.

To finish it off you can line it with either more hessian or any plain material.

Make and Wear

Child's Aran Jacket

Helen O'Sullivan, Derryquay Guild, Kerry

The pattern below should fit a 56cm chest, which is about age 3–4 years. The pattern panel is detailed separately and is worked twice across the back and once on each side of the front and on the sleeves.

You will need

400g Aran wool

1 pair of 3.75mm needles

1 pair of 4.5mm needles

Cable needle

Stitch holders

6 buttons

Tension

18 sts and 24 rows to 10cm over stocking stitch on 4.5mm needles

Pattern Panel: 29 sts and 24 rows to 11cm over stocking stitch on 4.5mm needles

Abbreviations

k = knit

p = purl

st(s) = stitch(es)

inc = increase

dec = decrease

inc p = increase once in next stitch purlwise

beg = beginning

patt = pattern

st st = stocking stitch

tog = together

sl1 = slip one stitch

psso = pass slipped stitch over

tbl = through back of loop

yfwd = yarn forward

CN = cable needle

C5F = slip next 2 stitches on to CN and hold in front of work, k3 then k2 from CN

C4F = slip next 2 stitches on to CN and hold in front of work, k2 then k2 from CN

C4B = as C4F but hold stitches at back of work

CpF = slip next 2 sts on to CN and hold in front of work, p1 then k2 from CN

CpB = slip next st on to CN and hold at back of work, k2 then p from CN

PATTERN PANEL	1st row: p2, k4, C5F, p6, k4, p2.

1st row: p2, k4, C5F, p6, k4, p2.

2nd row: k2, p4, k6, p5, k6, p4, k2.

3rd row: p2, C4F, p5, CpB, k1, CpF, p5, C4B, p2.

4th row: k2, p4, k5, p2, k1, p1, k1, p2, k5, p4, k2.

5th row: p2, k4, p4, CpB, k1, p1, k1, CpF, p4, k4, p2.

6th row: k2, p4, k4, p2, (k1, p1) twice, k1, p2, k4, p4, k2.

7th row: p2, C4F, p3, CpB, k1, (p1, k1) twice, CpF, p3, C4B, p2.

8th row: k2, p4, k3, p2, (k1, p1) 3 times, k1, p2, k3, p4, k2.

9th row: p2, k4, p2, CpB, k1, (p1, k1) 3 times, CpF, p2, k4, p2.

10th row: k2, p4, k2, p2, (k1, p1) 4 times, k1, p2, k2, p4, k2.

11th row: p2, C4F, p2, CpF, (p1, k1) 3 times, p1, CpB, p2, C4B, p2.

12th row: as 8th row.

13th row: p2, k4, p3, CpF, p1, (k1, p1) twice, CpB, p3, k4, p2.

14th row: as 6th row.

15th row: p2, C4F, p4, CpF, p1, k1, p1, CpB, p4, C4B, p2.

16th row: as 4th row.

17th row: p2, k4, p5, CpF, p1, CpB, p5, k4, p2.

18th row: k2, p4, k6, p2, k1, p2, k6, p4, k2.

19th row: p2, C4F, p6, C5F, p6, C4B, p2.

20th row: as 2nd row

These 20 rows form the pattern.

For the 9-stitch stocking stitch panel on the back between the 2 pattern panels put in a garter stitch every 6th row.

BACK

Using 3.75mm needles cast on 55 stitches.

1st row: *k1, p1, repeat from * to last stitch, k1.

2nd row: *p1, k1, repeat from * to last stitch, p1.

Continue until rib measures 5cm, ending with a 1st row.

Next row (inc row): p8, *inc p, p1, repeat from * to last 7 stitches, p7 (75 sts).

Change to 4.5mm needles and commence pattern.

1st row: k4, work 1st row of pattern panel for next 29 sts, k9, work 1st row of pattern panel for next 29 sts, k to end.

2nd row: p4, work 2nd row of pattern panel for next 29 sts, p9, work 2nd row of pattern panel for next 29 sts, p to end.

Continue incorporating the pattern panel, remembering to garter st every 6th row of the st st centre panel, until the work measures 21cm from beginning, ending with a wrong side row.

SHAPE RAGLAN
FOR SLEEVES

Cast off 5 sts at beg of next 2 rows (65 sts).

3rd row: k1, sl1, k1, psso, patt to last 3 sts, k2 tog, k1.

4th row: p2, patt to last 2 sts, p2.

Repeat 3rd and 4th rows 4 more times (55sts).

Next row: k1, sl1, k1, psso, patt to last 3 sts, k2 tog, k1.

Next row: p1, p2 tog, patt to last 3 sts, p2 tog tbl, p1 (51 sts).

Repeat last 2 rows 8 times more.

Leave remaining 19 sts on a holder.

SLEEVES

With 3.75mm needles cast on 29 sts and work 5cms of rib as given for back, ending with a 1st row.

Next row (inc row): p5, *inc p, p1, repeat from * until 5 stitches remain (39 sts).

Change to 4.5mm needles and commence pattern.

1st row: k5, work 1st row of pattern panel for next 29 sts, k to end.

2nd row: p5, work 2nd row of pattern panel for next 29 sts, p to end.

Keeping 29 sts at centre in patt and the remainder in st st (garter st every 6th row), continue working from 3rd row of patt panel, inc 1 stitch at each end of next and every following 4th row until 51 sts are on the needle.

Work without further shaping until sleeve measures 21cms or required length, ending with a wrong side row.

SHAPE TOP
OF SLEEVE

Cast off 5 sts at the beginning of next 2 rows.

3rd row: k1, sl1, k1, psso, pattern to last 3 sts, k2 tog, k1.

4th row: p2, patt to last 2 sts, p2.

Repeat 3rd and 4th rows 10 times (19 sts).

Next row: k1, sl1, k1, psso, patt to last 3 sts, k2 tog, k1.

Next row: p1, p2 tog, patt to last 3 sts, p2 tog tbl, p1.

Repeat these 2 rows twice more.

Leave remaining 7 sts on a holder.

JACKET LEFT FRONT

With 3.75mm needles cast on 25 sts and work in rib as described above for 5cms.

Next row (inc row): p2, inc p every other stitch until 36 sts.

Change to 4.5mm needles and commence pattern.

1st row: k4, work 1st row of patt panel for next 29 sts, k3.

2nd row: p3, work 2nd row of patt panel for next 29 sts, p to end.

Keeping 29 sts in patt panel and the remaining sts in st st (garter st every 6th row), continue working from 3rd row of patt panel until work measures same as back to raglan shaping, ending with a wrong side row.

SHAPE RAGLAN FOR SLEEVES

Next row: cast off 5 sts, patt to end.

Next row: patt to end.

1st row: k1, sl1, psso, patt to end.

2nd row: patt to last 2 sts, p2.

Repeat 1st and 2nd rows 4 times (26 sts).

Next row: k1, sl1, k1, psso, patt to end.

Next row: patt to last 3 sts, p2 tog tbl, p1.

Repeat last 2 rows (22 sts).

SHAPE NECK

Next row: k1, sl1, k1 psso, patt to end.

Next row: cast off 2 sts, patt to last 3 sts, p2 tog tbl, p1.

Work 5 rows, dec 1 st at raglan edge as before on every row. AT THE SAME TIME dec 1 st at neck edge on every row (8 sts).

Work 6 rows, dec 1 stitch at raglan edge only as before on every row (2 sts).

Next row: p2 tog tbl, fasten off.

JACKET RIGHT FRONT

With 3.75mm needles cast on 25 sts and rib as described above for 5cms.

Next row (inc row): p2, inc p every other stitch until 36 sts.

Change to 4.5mm needles.

1st row: k3, work 1st row of patt panel for next 29 sts, k to end.

2nd row: p4, work 2nd row of patt panel for next 29 sts, p to end.

Keeping 29 sts in patt panel and the remaining sts in st st, with every 6th row garter stitch as before, continue working from 3rd row of patt panel until work measures same as back to raglan shaping, ending with a right side row.

SHAPE RAGLAN FOR SLEEVES	Next row: Cast off 5 sts, patt to end.
	1st row: patt to last 3 sts, k2 tog, k1.
	2nd row: p2, patt to end.
	Repeat 1st and 2nd rows 4 times more (26 sts).
	Next row: patt to last 3 sts, k2 tog, k1.
	Next row: p1, p2 tog, patt to end.
	Repeat last 2 rows (22 sts).
SHAPE NECK	Next row: cast off 2 sts, patt to last 3 sts, k2 tog, k1.
	Next row: p1, p2 tog, patt to end.
	Complete as given for left side, working p2 tog instead of p2 tog tbl.
JACKET FRONT BANDS	With 3.75mm needles cast on 7 sts and work in rib as given for back until band is long enough when slightly pulled to reach up the front to neck shaping, ending with a second row.
	Leave sts on a safety pin.
	Sew band in place and mark positions for buttons.
	Work another band the same length making buttonholes as follows:
	Next row: (make buttonhole) rib 3, cast off 2 sts, rib to end.
	Next row: rib, casting on 2 sts over those cast off in previous row.
	Leave sts on a safety pin. Sew band in place.

NECK BAND

With size 3.75mm needles, and right side of work facing, rib across sts on right front band, pick up 13 sts up the right front neck, knit across sts on right sleeve, back and left sleeve, pick up 13 sts down left front neck and rib across left front band (73 sts).

Work 6 rows of rib. Cast off. Sew on buttons. Join side and sleeve seams.

Crochet Hats

Elaine Hynes, Castlebar Guild, Mayo

There are lots of patterns for crochet hats online, but these two are a great place to start. The band for the second hat (shown in photo) is simply a continuation of the pattern for 17 more rows. This can be done in a contrasting colour if you like. Once you have mastered the basic treble stitch the pattern is very easy to follow.

You will need

50g double knitting yarn for beanie *or* 100g for hat with band

3.5mm crochet hook

Abbreviations

ch = chain

ss = slip stitch

st = stitch

tr = treble

PATTERN ONE – FOR A BEANIE

To start, ch 4, join with ss into 1st ch st to form a ring. Ch 2 (counts as first treble), 9 tr into ring, ss to top of ch 2 to join (10 trebles).

1st round: ch 3, 1 tr into base of ch 3, 2 tr into each tr to end, ss into top of ch 3 (20 trebles).

2nd round: ch 3, 1 tr into next tr, 1 tr into next tr, *2 tr into next tr, 1 tr into next tr*. Repeat from * to *, ss into top of ch 3 (30 trebles).

3rd round: ch 3, 1 tr into next tr, 2 tr into next tr, 2 tr into space of fourth and fifth tr, *2 tr into next tr, 2 tr into space between next 2 tr*. Repeat from * to *, ss to top of ch 3 (40 trebles).

4th round: ss to space between first and second tr, ch 4, 1 tr into space between first and second tr, *1 tr, ch 1, 1 tr all into the same space between the next 2 tr*. Repeat from * to *, ss into ch 3 of ch 4.

5th round: ss to space between trs, ch 4, 1 tr into ch 1 space, (2 tr, ch 1, 2 tr) into next ch space, * (1 tr, ch 1, 1 tr) into next ch space, (2 tr, ch 1, 2 tr) into next ch space*. Repeat from * to *, ss into ch 3 of ch 4.

6th round: ss to space between tr, ch 3, (1 tr, ch 1, 2 tr) into chain space, *(2 tr, ch 1, 2 tr) into next chain space*. Repeat from * to *, ss into top of ch 3 (20 clusters).

Repeat 6th round until the hat is the desired length.

PATTERN TWO – FOR A HAT WITH A BAND

Follow pattern one, but repeat the 6th round 17 more times, then fold back.

Whirl Scarf

Anne Maria Dennison, Mainistir Na Féile Guild, Limerick

The yarn used in this scarf is made up of a mesh-like material so you can create an elaborate-looking scarf very simply. It comes in a wide range of colours and you can choose whichever colours take your fancy. There are several makes of yarn that produce slightly different effects, but they are all worked in the same way.

You will need

1 ball of 'whirl' yarn

4.5mm knitting needles

Open out the yarn, revealing a mesh-like, open-work yarn.

To cast on stitches, simply insert the needle into the first loop and each consecutive hole until 8 stitches have been picked up (see figure 1).

Using garter stitch, knit into each stitch to the end of the row, but instead of wrapping the whole thread around the needle, just pick up 1 loop from the top of the mesh (see figure 2). Be careful with this first row so as to establish the knitting pattern.

Unfold the yarn before each row and continue until the yarn has been almost all used.

Be sure to leave enough yarn to cast off – slip 1, knit 1 and pass the slipped stitch over the knit one.

As this is open work it must be handled very gently as stitches can slip off easily.

TIPS

Plastic needles work better than metal ones as stitches are less likely to slip off.

Use short needles in preference to long ones.

To make a longer narrower scarf just cast on 6 stitches instead of 8.

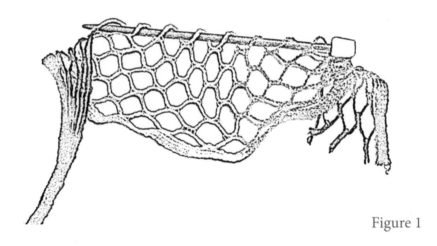

Figure 1

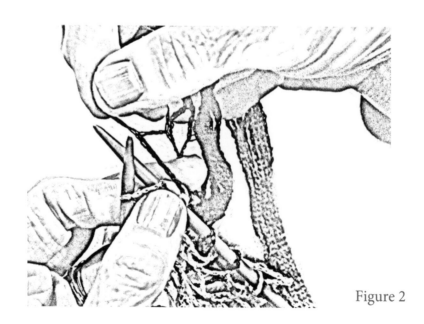

Figure 2

Upcycled Child's Skirt and Cap

Kay Murray, Broadford Guild, Clare

As I was preparing to send some clothes to a charity shop, my ten-year-old grand-daughter, Murielle, spotted an outdated wool pleated skirt and said she would love to wear one just like it. Adding pleats is a little fiddly but not difficult and you can find step-by-step instructions in a good sewing reference book.

I happened to have a pattern for a baseball cap at home also, so I made this to match.

You will need

Fully lined adult pleated skirt (or you could buy the lining material)

Zip

Iron-on interfacing for waist band and cap

5cm ribbon for inside band of cap (optional, see below)

Scissors

Sewing machine

Measuring tape

Baseball cap pattern (there are several available on the Internet, but the one I used was Simplicity pattern no. 8268)

SKIRT

Ascertain the waist measurement and length you require for the finished skirt.

Rip all the stitching from the original garment, except for the hem, and press the resulting material to remove the existing pleats.

Cut two pieces for the front and back of the skirt to the measurements required, ensuring you allow an extra centimetre on all edges for seams, as well as an extra 30cm for the pleats and retaining the original hem as the hem of your new skirt.

Insert a box pleat in the centre and two side pleats at each side of the centre box pleat in the front of the skirt.

Repeat the pleats on the back of the skirt.

With right sides facing, join the side seams and insert the zip on the left-hand side.

Cut the lining material to the right size – you don't need to allow for the pleats this time, but still need to include a seam allowance. Tack the lining to the waist of the skirt.

Cut out an 8cm-wide strip from the remaining material for the waist band. You may need to sew two strips together to make the appropriate length. Cut interfacing to the same size as the waist band and press to secure according to the instructions on the packet. With right sides facing sew the waist band to the outside of the top of the skirt and press and turn down a ½cm seam, then stitch to the skirt on the inside.

CAP

Cut out six wedge-shaped pieces of fabric for the crown and two crescent shapes for the peak, following your chosen pattern.

Cut six matching pieces of lining and six pieces of iron-on interfacing for the crown, and two pieces of interfacing for the peak.

Attach the interfacing to the inside of the crown pieces, following the instructions on the packet. Trim edges and sew all six pieces together to make a dome shape.

Sew the six pieces of lining together leaving one side open. Press the seams. Stitch the lining to the brim of the crown making sure the right side of the lining and right side of the crown are facing. Turn the cap right side out and stitch the open side of the lining on the inside of the finished cap.

Place the two interfaced peak pieces with right sides facing and stitch together along the outside of the crescent shape.

Turn right side out and ease out any wrinkles. Sew a seam 1cm in from the inside edge of the crescent shape. Make cuts in the fabric in towards the seam at 2cm intervals and use these flaps to sew the peak to the crown inside the cap.

Stitch a 5cm wide ribbon all around the inside of cap and turn in. Alternatively, you can use another strip of the skirt material cut on the bias, hemmed on one side and lined with interfacing.

Clones Lace Wild Rose Medallion Necklace

Brenda Leary, Blackrock Guild, Louth

I first tried making Clones lace in 2011, taking lessons from Maire Treanor, who has done great work in reviving this almost-forgotten style of crochet lace popular in the south-east Fermanagh and Monaghan areas since the famine period of 1847. I have used one of the most common motifs of this area, the wild rose, finishing it with a circle of Clones knots. I then fastened a chain of Clones knots to it to make it into a necklace.

You will need

1 x 20g ball each of no. 10 and 20 mercerised cotton thread

1.25mm crochet hook

Abbreviations

ch = chain

ss = slip stitch

dc = double crochet

tr = treble

pc = packing cord

WILD ROSE

Using No. 10 cotton, make 6 ch, ss into first ch to make a ring.

Make 5 ch, 1 tr into ring, (3 ch, 1 tr into ring) 3 times, ss to the first loop of the circle. You should have 5 bars radiating from the initial ring.

1st row of petals: (1 dc, 3 tr, 1 dc, ss into first space). Repeat into each space to make 5 petals.

Make 5 ch and ss around the back of the first of the ch bars radiating from the initial ring. Repeat this around each of the ch bars to make the base for the second row of petals.

2nd row of petals: make (1 dc, 5 tr, 1 dc, ss) around the first ch base you created. Repeat around each base. Make 7 ch and ss between the base of each of the petals you have created to make the base for the last row of petals.

3rd row of petals: Working each petal separately, *make 10 dc around first base of 7 ch. Turn. Make a loop of (4 ch, ss) into every second dc just made (5 loops). Turn and continue making 4 ch and ss into each loop of the previous row for 5 more rows, ending on front (left) side of the work. Work down the side of the petal to the base with 2 ch and ss into each loop. One petal is now complete, ss into centre.*

Ss into the next base of 7 ch and continue as for the first petal from * to * to make the next 4 petals.

PACKING CORD

This is used to edge the petals. Using No. 20 cotton, measure a length from hand to elbow and then double it. Cut. Make a ss through the fold using petal thread. Lay the doubled pc along the side of the petals as you crochet over it as follows:

Work up the side of a petal using 2 dc into each loop. In the top corner 1 dc, 5 tr, 1 dc into loop, then (1 dc, 3 tr, 1 dc) into each of the 3 middle loops, and 1 dc, 5 tr, 1 dc into last loop – 5 loops altogether. Remember to work over the pc, bringing it with you.

Work down the side of the petal in the same way as you worked up, 2 dc into each loop. Ss into bottom centre. Repeat for each of the petals.

When finished cut the pc close to the flower and finish off the thread.

(If you run out of pc, just cut more, double as before, join in and continue.)

THE CLONES KNOT | (This takes a little practice, so if you haven't done it before have a few trial runs before working around the rose!)

Use No. 20 thread. To make this knot crochet 6 chains. Put the thread over the needle as for a treble but at the thickest part of the needle. Swivel the hook clockwise to the left all the way round, then anti-clockwise to the right all the way round, catching the thread under the hook each time. Repeat for a total of 13 swivels. Bring the thread under the hook and pull it through all the loops made. Make ss on the top of the knot, then make 2 ch and ss on the left side of the knot. Gently pull the thread tight each time.

Edge the wild rose with Clones knots, making 3 across the top of each petal and 1 across the space between the petals. Make a chain of knots a little longer than the desired length (it will shrink slightly when washed). Attach the chain to the rose.

Wash the medallion in warm soapy water and rinse. This will tighten up all the stitches. Leave to dry flattened out face down on a towel. Press gently with a warm iron when dry.

Irish Crochet

Betty Teahan, Wicklow Town Guild, Wicklow

Irish crochet is a tradition that has been handed down through the generations and these patterns need some knowledge of the basic crochet stitches.

You will need

White cotton, varying from no. 20 to 150
(the higher the number the finer the thread)

Fine steel crochet hook

Padding cord

Abbreviations

ch = chain

dc = double crochet

dtr = double treble

htr = half treble

tr = treble

trtr = triple treble

sp = space

ss = slip stitch

Many intricate designs such as the rose and shamrock are used in Irish crochet. Traditionally picots are used in the background filling.

Quite often some stitches are worked over a cord, sometimes known as 'padding'. If you don't have cord try using two or three thicknesses of no. 5 or no. 10 cotton.

Once the piece is finished it should be washed. While still damp pin it out into shape – a large towel on the floor works well. Leave until dry. Don't iron crochet as it flattens the stitches.

ROSE SQUARE

Take 30cm of padding and form a small ring in the centre. Over the ring do 18 dc.

1st row: over cord do *1 dc, 1 htr, 5 tr, 1 htr, 1 dc*, 1 dc into the third dc of ring. Repeat from * to * five more times following with a dc into the sixth, ninth, twelfth, fifteenth and eighteenth dc of the initial ring respectively, ending with 1 ss into first dc. This gives you the first row of petals.

2nd row: over cord do petals of 1 dc, 1 htr, 7 tr, 1 htr, 1 dc, 1 dc into the back of dc between the petals of the former row.

3rd row: same as 2nd row but putting 9 tr instead of 7 tr into each petal. Cut cord.

4th row: ss to second tr on petal, 1 dc, *5 ch, 1 dc into sixth tr, 5 ch, 1 dc into second tr of next petal*. Repeat from * to * end of round, ending with ss into first dc.

5th row: ss into 5 ch loop, 3 ch, 2 tr, 3 ch, 3 tr into same loop, *(5 ch, 1 dc into next loop) twice, 5 ch, 3 tr into next loop, 3 ch, 3 tr into same loop*. Repeat from * to *, ss into third chain at start. The piece should now be square.

6th row: ss to 3 ch sp, 3 ch, 2 tr, 3 ch, 3 tr into same loop, *(5 ch, 1 dc into next loop) 3 times, 5 ch, 3 tr, 3 ch, 3 tr into 3 ch sp*. Repeat from * to *, ss into third chain at start of row.

Continue with this pattern adding an extra 5 ch loop to each side until the square is the required size.

LARGE
TRADITIONAL
FLOWER

Wind padding cord 10 times around a 6mm cable needle.

1st row: work 35 dc into ring. Turn work.

2nd row: work 35 tr into dc.

3rd row: (2 ch, 1 dc) between each tr.

4th row: (3 ch, 1 dc) into each 2 ch loop.

5th row: (3 ch, 1 dc) into each 3 ch loop.

6th row: (4 ch, 1 dc) into each 3 ch loop.

7th row: cut 90cm of padding cord (2 strands of no. 10 cotton), work 35 little fans of 1 dc, 1 htr, 3 tr, 1 htr, 1 dc, worked over cord only, attaching between each with 1 dc into 4 ch loop.

8th row: without cord and behind fans, work trtr into each 4 ch loop of the 6th row with 1 ch in between each (68 in all).

9th and 10th row: 3 ch, dc into each chain space.

11th row: on 4-strand cord (115cm or a little more) work 3 dc in each loop.

12th row: work 5 petals as follows: 20 dc over cord, turn, 20 dc without cord into the previous 20, turn, 20 dc into the previous ones. Take up the cord and finish the petal with 20 more dc over cord into the last 20.

Then do 3 petals with the same 20 dc over cord at either side, but two rows of 6 x 3 ch loops instead of the 2 rows of dc, in the centre, attached with a dc to every 3rd dc in the first row, and to the ch loop in the 2nd row. After the last petal do 15 dc around the centre over cord.

Work 3 hooks as follows:

1st hook: over cord only work 60 dc. Mark 34th dc for joining the tip of the hook, attach at the marked point with ss, work 60 back down over cord and into the first 60.

2nd hook: work 80 dc over cord, join to the first hook for the first 30 dc. Mark 54th dc for joining the tip of the hook; work back down as above.

3rd hook: as 1st hook, joining to centre one for first 30 dc.

Work 15 dc around the centre over cord. Work 3 petals with chain centres as above, then 5 solid petals.

Work dc around the centre over cord to the first petal.

A stem can be added later if you wish.

Peyote Stitch Bracelet

Wanda McCamley, Delgany Guild, Wicklow

People have always loved beads and beading. Beads have been discovered dating back 40,000 years. Over time they have been made from many materials, including bone, shell, gold, silver and semi-precious stones. It is worth buying good quality beads as they are generally more even. Don't use any that are unusually big or small.

You will need

For an 18 cm bracelet:

10g size 8 beads (tubular beads work well for this pattern, but almost any size beads will do as long as they are evenly sized)

Beading needle

Matching nylon beading thread (Nymo D would be good)

Toggle clasp

Beading mat (a beading mat is inexpensive and is excellent for preventing beads from rolling away)

Tip out some beads onto the beading mat and put the lid back on the container!

Thread the needle with 1½ metres of beading thread. (Stretching the thread and pulling it through beeswax or Thread Heaven will help to prevent it tangling.)

1st row: thread on 1 bead and, leaving a 25cm tail, sew through the bead 2 more times to keep it from slipping. Add on 5 more beads. Hold these 6 beads firmly between your thumb and first finger; put the thread over that finger and hold it in place with your middle finger.

2nd row: work from right to left; hold your work firmly and tighten your thread after each bead is added. There will be 3 beads on each row. With your needle pick up 1 new bead and, skipping the 1st bead of the 1st row, sew through the 2nd. Pick up 1 bead, miss the 3rd bead and sew through the 4th. Pick up 1 bead, miss the 5th and sew through the 6th. Turn your work. (Working from right to left the 2nd, 4th and 6th beads will now be sitting up higher. The next 3 beads will fit into the spaces – this row can be a bit squiggly! Don't take fright.)

At the end of the row pull one thread up and one down and if necessary manoeuvre the beads into position (see figure 1).

Repeat row 2 until the desired length is reached.

Turn your work.

ADDING TOGGLE

Sew into the bead below the one the thread has just come from and work through your beads coming out of the middle bead on the last row (see figure 2).

Pick up 4 beads; sew through one end of your toggle; pick up 4 more beads and sew through the middle bead of the second last row and then through the middle bead of the last row (see figure 3).

Sew through all these beads several times to strengthen the fastening. Weave in your thread as follows:

Leaving the end of your thread 15 to 20cm long (it's so much easier) sew back into your beadwork following a path between and through your beads. (Use good light and make sure the thread doesn't show as this will spoil your work.) Tie 2 or 3 half-hitch knots as you go. Sew through a few more beads and cut the thread. (If you need to add a new thread in the middle of your beading reverse the procedure and make sure you join in the middle of a row.)

Repeat at other end with the second half of the toggle.

TIPS

Try not to pierce your worked thread with your needle as this can prevent your bead from falling into place.

To undo a stitch: take your thread out of your needle, because it is so easy to split a thread and this can be nearly impossible to fix. (Much more difficult than re-threading your needle!)

Figure 1

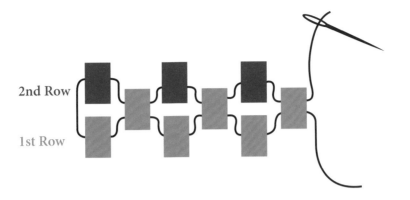

2nd Row

1st Row

Figure 2

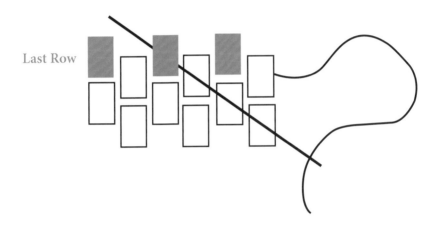

Last Row

Figure 3

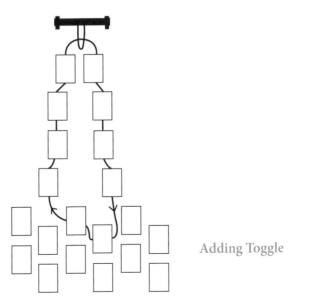

Adding Toggle

93

Beaded Ring Necklace

Margaret Clince, Garristown Guild, Dublin

Ring component design by Nikia Angel as featured in
Easy Crystal Stitching

Learning to make your own jewellery opens up so many possibilities for creating beautiful gifts, or pieces to match your wardrobe!

You will need

For each ring:

  108 x size 11 seed beads (A)

  18 x 4mm crystal bicones (B)

  1 x 18mm crystal rivoli

Size 10 beading needle

Beading thread

Necklace clasp

Round 1: on a length of thread string (3A and 1B) 9 times. Leave a 15cm tail and tie in a knot to form a ring. Pass the needle through the first 2 A beads again (see figure 1).

Round 2: add 5A beads, skip 3 beads and pass through the next A in round 1. Repeat to add a total of 9 nets attaching 5A nets to the centre As of 3A sets in round 1. Exit from 3rd A added in this round (see figure 2).

Round 3: string 1B and pass through the centre A of the next net of round 2. Repeat to add a total of 9B (see figure 3). Tighten up the thread and ensure the beads form a snug circle in the centre of the ring. Pass the thread through this round again and exit from a middle A of a 3A set in round 1.

Round 4: repeat round 2 (see figure 4).

Round 5: add rivoli and repeat round 3. As you fit the beads together snuggly they will hold the rivoli in place.

When you have several of these rings in the same or contrasting colours arrange them together in a pattern that appeals to you. Stitch them together through 2 or 3 beads on the side of each ring.

When all the rings are connected start to make the chain by first taking up the top 3 beads from one of the outside rings. I used 2 needles and took up 3 A beads on each needle, then passed them both through a B bead. Continue until the desired length is reached, then add one end of the clasp. Repeat for the other side.

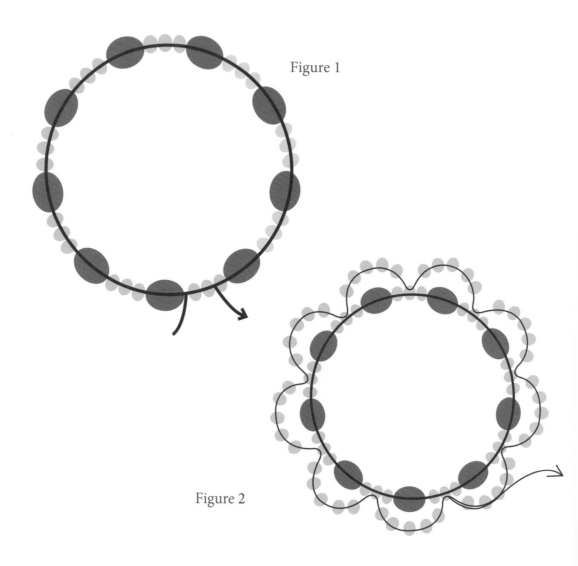

Figure 1

Figure 2

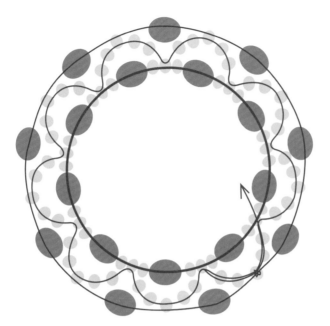

Figure 3

Figure 4

Tissue Paper Pompom

You will need

Coloured tissue paper

Florists/garden wire

Scissors

Fishing wire or ribbon

Lay out 16 pieces of 50 x 75cm coloured tissue paper in a stack.

Make 4–5cm folds parallel to the short side all the way along, creasing each fold accordion style.

Wrap one end of the wire around the centre of the tissue paper and the other around the end of a pen to make a circle shape.

With a sharp scissors trim the ends of the tissue paper into either a semi-circle petal shape or a pointed shape.

Separate each layer of tissue paper one layer at a time, pulling them away from the centre.

Once your pompom is fully fluffed out, hang with fishing wire or ribbon using the hook you made earlier in the wire.

To make a smaller pompom use 10 sheets of paper, 50 x 38cm.

Donegal Tweed Necklace and Ring

Maura Riordan, Dun Laoghaire Guild, Dublin

Create beautiful necklaces and rings from small pieces of interesting fabric. I used Donegal tweed to make a variety of motifs, which I strung together with some small beads for the necklace and attached to a suitable finding for a matching ring.

You will need

Tweed fabric

Beads or buttons

Needle and thread

Necklace wire

Curved tube/pipe beads and small pearls

Necklace clasp and crimps

Ring finding

Jewellery pliers

Cardboard for templates

Make circular cardboard templates in two or three different sizes (I used 8cm and 11cm circles for the necklace shown here).

Cut out a selection of circles from the tweed in different sizes. Contrasting fabrics could be used.

Fold the edge of each circle over about 3mm and tack around the entire edge of the circle to gather. Pull the thread to gather into the centre, then press down into shape and tie off.

Sew the different-sized gathered circles on top of one another and finish by stitching beads or buttons to the centre.

Assemble the circles. This can be done in a variety of ways. In the sample necklace they were stitched to wire and the necklace was completed with silver pipe beads and small pearls. The circles could also be sewn together.

Sew one of the circles securely to the ring finding.

A clasp can easily be attached to your necklace by using crimp beads. Insert two crimp beads onto the wire followed by the clasp. Take the end of the wire and fold it back through the crimp beads. Using your pliers compress your crimps.

Felted Bead Necklace

Maura Riordan, Dun Laoghaire Guild, Dublin

Felting is the process of turning wool into a dense hard fibre – felt. Making felt beads is relatively easy. There are two methods – wet felting and needle felting. I have combined both in this project.

You will need

Unspun merino wool
– available in a vast
assortment of colours

Liquid soap
(approx. 2 tbsps of shavings
of any soap dissolved in
100mls of hot water and
topped up to 500mls with
warm water)

Towel

Felting needle

Hot and cold water

Beading needle

Necklace wire or cotton
thread

Necklace clasp and crimps

Jewellery pliers

Pull some of the wool fibre apart. Roll the fibres into a ball at different angles.

Some needle felting is helpful at this stage to form the bead. Needle felting involves pushing a barbed needle through the wool fibres, which causes them to lock as the needle agitates the wool. This method is good for surface design as it allows you to felt layers of different coloured wool together. This allows you to make multicoloured beads if desired.

Cover the surface you are working at with a folded towel, as this is where it gets messy!

Now dip the ball into a bowl of very hot soapy water.

Start to massage the ball around in the palms of your hands.

Repeat the process of dipping into the hot soapy water and rolling until you can feel the bead shape firming up a little. Continue the process until your ball has become firm. After a few minutes your wool ball should be looking more like a felt ball. Rinse it in cold water.

Repeat the process until you have the number of beads you require. Allow the beads to dry. With practice you should get the hang of how much pressure is required for the bead to come together and how much wool is needed to make the size of bead you require. So, while your first few beads may be a little uneven, you will quickly have a selection of colourful beads lined up ready to go.

Now assemble your necklace by threading the needle with necklace wire or cotton thread. You can alternate your felt beads with other kinds of beads if you like. Necklace wire and clasps are all readily available in bead shops or online, and you will need a small pair of jewellery pliers to attach the clasp to the wire or thread.

Button Rings

Maura Riordan, Dun Laoghaire Guild, Dublin

This is a lovely way to showcase any vintage buttons in your collection. Every piece will be unique and you can let your imagination run wild!

You will need

Buttons – a variety of sizes and colours

Assortment of beads

Ring findings (ensure they are suitable for sewing buttons to and have a flat top for the buttons to sit securely)

Needle and transparent nylon thread

Select three or four buttons of different sizes and complementary colours.

Stack them as desired.

Using a needle and the nylon thread assemble the buttons. Ensure each stitch goes through to your ring finding. Seed beads or small pearls can also be attached. In this method the buttons are securely fixed to the ring without the use of glue.

Store and Keep

Lumra Bag

Réiltín MacCana, Dun Laoghaire Guild, Dublin

Lumra, the Irish word for fleece, is a uniquely Irish craft using sheep's fleece in its natural colours of white, brown and grey to make floor rugs, bags, wall hangings, cushion tops and tea cosies. Designs should be simple and geometric in style to suit the character of the canvas. This bag uses a Navajo Native American design, but Celtic Fret designs also work well. A raw skirted fleece will need to be washed in a soda solution, rinsed well and dried (in a pillow case) in the open air. It must then be carded. Some woollen mills supply prepared fleeces, usually referred to as 'tops'.

You will need

Sheep's fleece – washed and carded in at least two colours

Matching 6-ply wool for plait around the edges.

5½mm crochet hook or locker needle

Locking wool (if using the locker needle method)

Rug canvas 3 H.P.I.

Strong thread and sewing needle

Darning needle (for binding edges)

Graph paper and coloured pencils

Contrasting threads (for charting design on canvas)

Lining material

Bamboo bag handles

PREPARATION OF LUMRA WOOL

Take a length of carded wool about 45cm long and gradually tease it out to finger thickness.

Carefully wind this over the back of one hand, twisting with the other hand as you go.

Repeat twice or three times, making a fairly firm rope. Assemble several of these before starting to work.

PREPARATION OF CANVAS

Cut the canvas bigger than the size you need. Fold to the correct size taking the turn into account. Turn in all sides about 3cm and secure with a back stitch. Make sure that all holes, particularly at the corners, are aligned when folded and completely visible.

Bind all the sides using plaited stitch or long-legged cross stitch (I used the latter) and two strands of 6-ply wool.

DESIGN	Plot the design on graph paper using coloured pencils. Transfer the main points to canvas using coloured thread in the matching holes. The design may be stitched now or included later in the main body of the work.
CROCHET HOOK METHOD – THE TRADITIONAL ONE	Start in the top right-hand corner of the prepared canvas and work right to left. Hold a strand of prepared wool in one hand underneath the canvas. Insert the hook from the right side and draw up a loop about 1cm high. Roll back slightly before withdrawing the hook in a downward movement. Move onto the next hole in the canvas and draw up another loop and work across the canvas in this manner, changing colour as dictated by your design. To join wool tease (splice) the ends together. To finish, break the wool short and tease the end into the second last stitch.
LOCKER NEEDLE METHOD	This is the method I used for the bag shown. It is preferred as it is more economical with wool as a smaller loop suffices and a more even finish is easier and quicker to achieve. However, a locking wool is required and this *must* be carried with every stitch and started and finished securely. Thread the needle with a strand of locking wool, Báinín is good, and attach it firmly to the canvas. Attach the end of a strand of Lumra securely also.
	Start in the top right-hand corner of the prepared canvas and work right to left. Pass the needle up through the canvas from the underside, drawing up a workable length of locking wool. Pass the needle downwards through the next hole and draw up a loop of lumra wool. Carry the loop on the hook and proceed in the same manner to the following holes until there are 8–10 loops on the hook.

Draw the needle and the locking wool through the loops, thus locking them on the top side of the canvas.

When the first strand of locking wool is used up, cut a new length and stitch it on, thus avoiding knots in the work. Join fresh lengths of lumra wool by teasing (splicing) the ends together.

When turning corners or starting a new row take the needle and locking wool through the back of the canvas and up again through the hole in the next row.

To finish, break the lumra wool short. Bend and hook upwards beside the second-last stitch. Fasten the locking wool securely to the canvas.

ASSEMBLING THE
BAG

Cut a piece of lining fabric approximately 5cm longer and wider than the completed panel of lumra work. Turn in a 2.5cm hem and sew to the edges of the canvas with strong matching thread. Fold in half and join the sides together using buttonhole stitch. Affix handles to the top.

Leather Bag

Statia Ivers, Ballycoog Guild, Wicklow

Making your own bag is much simpler than you might think! You can get many different patterns in a good craft shop or on the Internet and can incorporate all sorts of decorative designs with a simple leather tool.

You will need

Bag pattern

Tooling leather

Leather thonging

Leather needle

Fasteners

Lining material

Punch tool (an implement that looks a little like a blunt screwdriver with a rounded end)

Stanley knife and cutting board

Skiving tool

Slicker wheel

Place the pattern onto the leather, mark and cut out.

Trace the design onto the right side of the leather with a blunt-ended pencil and go over each line with the punch tool. Patterns will often come with a design, but you can also create your own.

Lightly dampen the leather with a sponge. Don't soak it as it might leave a stain.

Holding the leather in one hand and the tool in the other with the right side of the leather facing you, push up the area between the lines from the back by rubbing evenly with the tool; continue until the design can be seen on the right side of the leather.

Line the inside of the bag and attach fasteners.

Punch holes all around the bag and sew the pieces of the bag together with the thonging.

Cut the strap from the leather, as long or short as you wish. Skive the edges of the strap to give a more rounded look and polish with a slicker wheel. Use rivets or stitching to attach the strap to the bag.

Covered File Box

Helen Weir, Two-Mile-House Guild, Kildare

Covering a file box was an adaptation of making a padded box, which I had the opportunity to learn at the Kildare Federation Craft Day.

You will need

Old file box

½m upholstery fabric

½m lining fabric

Thin wadding

Some strong cardboard
(a cereal packet will do)

Sharp scissors

Pencil and ruler

Copydex glue

Metal corners
(optional – available in craft stores or online)

Note: The green box in the photograph was made by Helen Weir and the red ones are by Statia Ivers of Bally-coog Guild.

Carefully take all the plastic bits off the box – my hubbie and his tools had more success at this than I did. This box had a spring grip inside and a hook on the spine. (You can leave the closing mechanism and button in place – it just takes a bit of time later in cutting around and leaving enough of the material to tuck under the plastic to finish it neatly.)

Place the box on the upholstery material. Cut a shape from the material, leaving enough to cover and overlap the front edge, bottom, rear and side edges of the box (with an overlap for the front and side edges) and the lid (with a slight overlap for the inside of the lid) (see figure 1).

Using Copydex glue (this should dry out without marking the material if applied thinly), cover the front edge, bottom, rear edge and lid of the box. Place the box on the material and pull up and smooth the front edge. Then close the box and smooth the material on the bottom, working your way to the rear edge. Do the same to this and the lid of the box making sure there are no wrinkles.

The glue can dry quickly, so work until finished. If you have left the closing mechanism cut some lines over the buttons (like a star *) – the plastic should pop through – then push the triangles

117

under the plastic with a knife blade (you may need to trim off a little of the material).

Before gluing the inside edges cut a rectangle out of the corners of the material (see figure 1) so that when they are put in place they are not too bulky and glue the remaining edges of the material at both front and back. Open the lid and put a little glue on the inside front edge and fold and smooth the overlap in place.

Make straight cuts in the material on either side of the line where the lid folds. Now fold the edge of the material on one side of the lid inside – before gluing in place make sure the corner edge is folded neatly on itself. Repeat on the other side of the lid.

Now the only sides left are those of the main box. By folding the front vertical edge onto itself by a quarter of an inch and then gluing the material in place and securing the overlap inside the box, you can make a neat edge at the front of the box (see figure 2). Repeat this on the sides. The outside is complete.

Measure the inside base of the box and cut out two card rectangles slightly smaller than the base. Then measure the length of the long and short sides and again cut out two card rectangles slightly smaller than each size. (It is important that the templates are not too big so that once they are covered with material they will fit in the box.)

Cut out wadding to cover each card template and glue in place.

Place each template on the lining fabric and cut a rectangle of material for each that will cover one side with an overlap.

Place the material right side down and put the template on it, wadding side down. Cut squares from the edges of the material, but do not cut all the way to the card corner (the material will fray). Put glue on the edges of the card and fold the material over and secure in place once the corners are neat. Repeat this on all templates.

Glue one of the large bases in the bottom of the box, material facing up, then put some glue on the sides and place them in position – you may have to hold them in place until the glue dries a little. The main box is now complete with a padded lining.

The last rectangle is for the inside of the lid and should be glued in place. (You can also make a third padded rectangle and put it on top of the lid to make that cushioned too.)

Add metal corners if using.

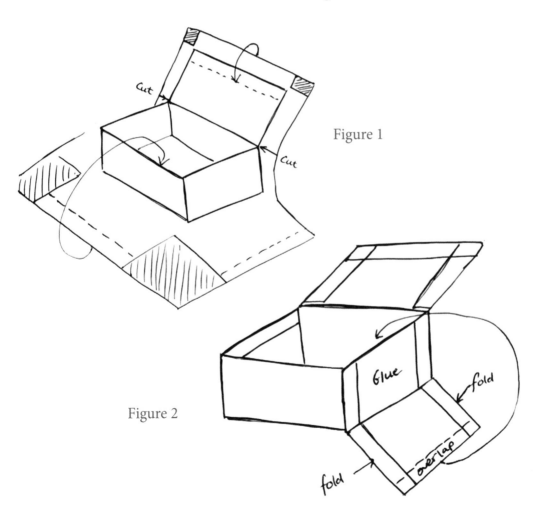

Figure 1

Figure 2

119

Hedgerow Basket

Betty Gorman, Castletown Guild, Laois

If you are lucky enough to live in the country like I do, you can cut your own sally rods to make a hedgerow basket. You need to completely dry out the rods before starting your basket and then rehydrate them – if you don't do this, the rods will shrink later and your weave will become loose.

You will need

Sharp pruners

Stanley knife

Weight or stone to hold down the bottom

Bundle of sally or willow rods (steep them the day before and keep them moist while you work by rolling them in a damp towel)

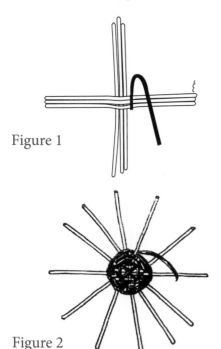

Figure 1

Figure 2

To start the bottom you need 6 strong thick rods. Cut a slit in the centre of 3 of the rods. This should be just big enough to run the other 3 through. Space them out into a cross formation (see figure 1).

Inserting a thin, flexible rod into the slit in the centre, weave in and out through the rods. This will force the rods into 12 spokes which form the frame of the base (see figure 2). To add a new base rod, just place the new one next to the old one and continue weaving.

Once the base is the required size, insert 2 thick rods each side of each of the base rods (24 rods) and bend them upright. Trim off the ends of the base rods at this point.

Put the weight on the bottom to help keep it firmly in place. Insert a weaving rod next to one of the thicker side rods and start weaving up the side of the basket. Continue to the required height.

Use a 3 and 2 plait to finish off the top of the basket (see figure 3). Cut 6 guide canes (lengths of rod about 15cm long) and insert them beside the first 6 uprights. Bend each upright over the guide cane and plait the uprights together along the top of the basket as illustrated. When the sixth cane is reached cut off the first upright, from underneath on the outside of the basket. Incorporate the next upright and continue to plait, incorporating each upright as you reach it, and trimming the shortest one off as you pick up each new one. When you reach the start point, thread the last uprights through the start of the plait, replacing the guide canes with these last uprights. Trim the ends.

To make handles twist 3 long fine rods together. Insert one end under the plait between 2 of the upright rods, pushing through to bring both ends of the twist together. Twist the two halves of the handle together and then insert the end under the sixth upright along from the original insertion point. Thread the handle down through the weaving to the bottom of the basket. Trim the ends. Do the same on the opposite side for the other handle.

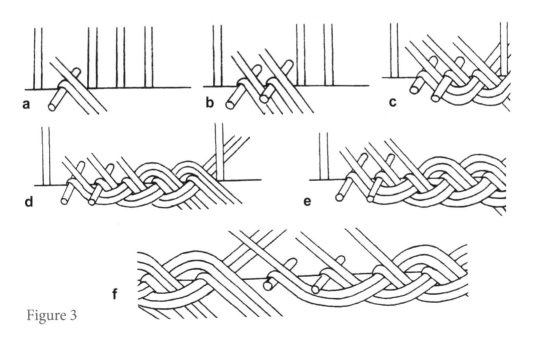

Figure 3

123

Rushwork Coil Table Mat

Betty Gorman, Castletown Guild, Laois

I cut and saved the rushes in the photo many years ago from the River Gowel near Grantstown Lake, Co. Laois. Bullrushes are used for this kind of work. Harvest them in March or April and stand upright in a dry, airy shed for about 3 months. Shake off any mould that grows and they are ready to use. They can also be bought from specialist suppliers.

You will need

Large bundle of rushes

Embroidery needle

Strong thread

Clear wood varnish

Soak the rushes for about half an hour before starting to work. Keep them moist by wrapping in a wet towel.

Make a plait with the rushes in the same way as you would plait hair. Coil the plait into a circular shape (see figure 1).

Stitch firmly through each coil and as you approach the end thin out the plait so that it marries easily into the coil. Stitch to secure the ends.

This can be made as small or as big as required.

Take great care to hide stitching that passes through the rushes. Fasten off securely.

Varnish 2 or 3 times to form a waterproof surface.

Figure 1

Hand Stamped Tea Towel

You will need

Plain white tea towel or cotton fabric

Fabric paints

Potatoes

Cookie cutters

Place your cookie shape of choice on top of your potato and press firmly so that your cookie shape makes an indent in the potato.

Cut around the shape of the cookie cutter to reveal the shape in the potato. (You can also create a shape free-hand with a knife, e.g. a triangle.)

Place a piece of cardboard between your tea towel and your surface so that the paint doesn't seep through.

Place your stamps in the fabric paint colour of your choice and stamp away.

Hang up on a clothes line to dry overnight. If you've been using cotton fabric add a hem to complete the tea towel.

Celebrate

Lace Crochet Baby Bonnet and Bootees

Maureen Neary, Brickens Guild, Mayo

These beautiful baby clothes are destined to become family heirlooms. The basic crochet stitches can be combined in fine thread to produce a very impressive project.

You will need

BONNET

1 ball no. 10 cotton crochet thread

1.75mm steel crochet hook

160cm narrow ribbon

BOOTEES

1 ball no. 10 cotton crochet thread

1.75mm steel crochet hook

90cm narrow ribbon

Abbreviations

ch = chain

dc = double crochet

ss = slip stitch

sp = space

st = stitch

tr = treble

BONNET

To start: 6 ch, join with ss to form a ring.

Round 1 (right side): ch 3, 2 tr into ring, ch 2 (3 tr, 2 ch) in ring 5 times, join with ss to top of 3 ch (18 trs). At the end of round 1 place a coloured marker to show right side.

Round 2: ss into next tr, 3 ch, tr in same st and in next tr, 2 tr in next ch sp, ch 2, skip next tr, *2 tr in next tr, tr in next tr, 2 tr in next 2 ch sp, ch 2, skip next tr*. Repeat from * to * until the end of the round, join with ss to first tr (30 trs).

Rounds 3–9: ss into next tr, ch 3, tr in same st and in each tr to next 2 ch space, 2 tr in 2 ch space, ch 2, skip next tr, *2 tr in next tr, tr in each tr to next 2 ch space, 2 tr in 2 ch space, ch 2, skip next tr*. Repeat from * to *, join with ss to first tr (114 trs).

Round 10: ch 1, dc in same st and in each tr to next 2 ch space, *2 dc in 2 ch space, dc in each tr to next 2 ch space*. Repeat from * to * until the end of the round, 3 dc in last 2 ch space, join with ss to first dc (127 dc). Do not finish off.

Row 1 (eyelet row): ss in 5 dc, ch 6 (counts as first tr plus 3 ch now and throughout), skip next 3 dc, tr in next dc (ch 3, skip next 3 dc, tr in next dc) to end of row (29 spaces).

Row 2: turn, ss in first 3 ch space, (3 ch tr, 2 ch, 2 tr) at base of this 3 ch (this forms first shell), (3 ch, skip next 3 ch space, work shell in next 3 ch space across) to end of row.

Rows 3–13: turn, (3 ch, tr, 2 ch, 2 tr) (shell), (3 ch, skip next 3 ch space, work shell – 2 tr, 2 ch, 2 tr in each shell to end. Continue in pattern until row 13 is completed.

Ch 1, do not turn, work 27 dc evenly spaced across end

rows of crown to back, dc in next 10 dc across back, work 27 dc evenly spaced across other end rows of crown.

Do not finish off.

NECK BAND

Row 1 (eyelet round): ch 6, do not turn, skip next 2 dc, tr in next dc, (ch 3, skip next 3 dc, tr in next dc) 15 times (16 3 ch spaces).

Row 2: ch 1, turn, dc in first tr (3 dc in next 3 ch space, dc in next tr) to end (65 dc).

Row 3: ch 1, turn, dc in first dc, ch 3, skip next 2 dc, dc in next 2 dc (ch 3, skip next dc, dc in next 2 dc) across to last 3 dc, skip next 2 dc, dc in last dc.

Finish off.

TO FINISH

Weave a 90cm length of ribbon through eyelet row of neck band. Sew a ribbon rose to each corner.

Weave a 70cm ribbon through eyelet row of crown and tie in a bow at the back.

BOOTEE

SOLE

Work 22 ch loosely.

Round 1 (right side): 7 tr in fourth ch from hook, tr in each ch across to last ch, 8 tr in last ch. Working in front loop of ch tr in each of 17 chs, join with ss to top of beginning ch (50 tr). At the end of round 1, place a coloured marker to show right side.

Round 2: ch 3, tr in first tr, 2 tr in each of next 7 tr, tr in next

17 tr, 2 tr in next 8 tr, tr in each tr around, join with ss to first tr (66 tr).

Round 3: ch 3, tr in first tr, 2 tr in next tr, (tr in next tr, 2 tr in next tr) 6 times, tr in next 18 tr, 2 tr in next tr, (tr in next tr, 2 tr in next tr) 7 times, tr in next 10 tr (place a marker around last tr made for joining placement), tr in last 8 tr, join with ss to first tr. Finish off (82 trs).

INSTEP

Work 13 ch loosely.

Row 1 (right side): tr in fourth ch from hook and in each ch across to last ch, 8 tr in last ch. Working in front loops of beginning ch, tr in next 10 chs (28 tr).

Row 2: ch 4, turn, skip next tr, tr in next tr, (ch 1, skip next tr, tr in next tr) 4 times, (ch 1, tr in next tr) 7 times, (ch 1, skip next tr, tr in next tr) 5 times (17 1 ch spaces).

Row 3: ch 3, turn, (tr in next 1 ch space and in next tr) 5 times, (2 tr in next 1 ch space, tr in next tr) 8 times, (tr in next 1 ch space and in next tr) 4 times. Ch 39 loosely, being careful not to twist ch, join with ss to first tr.

Do not finish off (43 trs).

SIDES

Round 1 (right side): ch 3, tr in next tr and in each tr and in each ch around, join with ss to first tr (82 tr).

Round 2: ch 3, tr in next tr and in each tr around, join with ss to first tr.

Round 3: ch 3, tr in next tr and in each tr around and join with ss to first tr.

Do not finish off.

JOINING

Ch 1 with **wrong** side of sides and sole together, matching first tr of sides with marked tr of sole and working on inside loops of **both** pieces, dc in same st and in each tr around, join with ss to first dc.

Finish off.

CUFF

Round 1: with **right** side facing, toe of bootee to right, working in free loops of ch on row 3 of sides and in ends of rows of instep, join thread with ss in first free ch, ch 1, dc in same st and in each ch across, work 13 dc evenly across, join with ss to first dc (52 dc).

Round 2 (eyelet row): ch 4, skip next dc, (tr in next dc, skip next dc, ch 1, skip next dc) around. Join with ss to first tr (26 1 ch spaces).

Round 3: ss in next 1 ch space, ch 3, (tr, ch 2, 2 tr) in same sp, ch 3, skip next 1 ch space, (work shell – 2 tr, 2 ch, 2 tr – in next 1 ch space, ch 3, skip next 1 ch space) around, join with ss to first tr (13 shells).

Rounds 4–6: work beginning shell, ch 3 (work shell in next shell, ch 3) around, join with ss to first tr.

Round 7: ss in next tr and in next 2 ch space, (dc, ch 3, dc) in same sp and in each 3 ch space and each shell around, join with ss to first dc.

Finish off.

Weave 45cm length of ribbon through eyelet row.

Sew ribbon rose to centre of instep.

Make another bootee the same.

Happy Christmas

Iris Folding

Maura Davis, Delgany Guild, Wicklow

Iris folding, also known as abstract paper quilting, is a relatively new craft that originated in Holland around the turn of the millennium.

The iris consists of colourful strips of paper that fill up the pattern from the outside to the inside and join in the middle, just as the iris of your eye encloses the pupil. It's a very simple technique with wonderful results. I have given a basic triangle template here, which has been used to make a Christmas card. Once you have completed that project you can find plenty more patterns on the Internet.

You will need

Card paper

Scrap paper in three complementary colours (I would recommend 2 plain and 1 patterned)

Holographic paper such as that used for wine bottle bags

Sticky tape

Double-sided tape

Scissors

Iris folding template

Copy or trace the template onto a large sheet of paper for your pattern. Trace the outline of the template onto your card and cut out and discard the triangle shape. Place the card face down over the pattern so that it shows through the triangle-shaped opening and stick in place with a piece of masking tape on one side, so that you can lift it up as you work to check how your pattern appears on the right side.

Cut your scrap paper into strips about 2cm wide and slightly longer than the longest side of the pattern. Fold each strip in half lengthwise.

Place the first strip of paper over the section numbered 1 in the pattern, with the fold running along the side nearest the centre. Stick it to the card at both ends with tape and trim any extra that might hang over the side of the card. Take a contrasting piece of paper and do the same thing for section 2 in the pattern and repeat with your third colour for section 3. Continue covering the pattern sections in numerical order alternating the colours as you go. (More complex patterns will list which colour should be used for each numbered segment.)

To finish, cut a piece of holographic paper big enough to cover the unnumbered section at the centre of the pattern and stick it face down. Flip the card over and you will see your finished design.

Remove the pattern and stick your card to another piece of card with double-sided tape and add any further embellishments you like, such as the star and pot shown in the photograph.

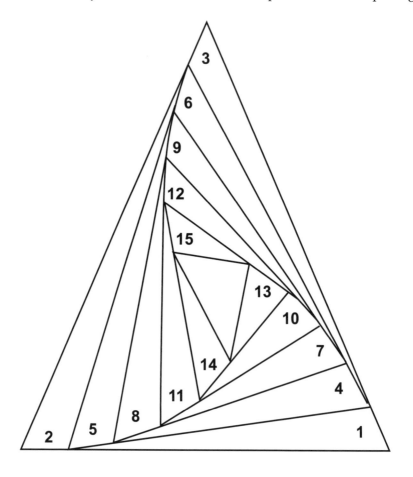

Template of basic triangle

Thank You

DIY Circular Disc Banner

You can make this banner with hearts, snowflakes or other patterns if you have the right paper punches. Craft paper punches are widely available in craft shops or online.

You will need

Coloured card

5cm circle punch

White thread

Sewing machine

Choose a colour theme for your disc banner and the order in which you would like to display the colours.

Using your circle punch, punch out about 20 circles per colour.

Stack your colours in separate piles so that they are within easy reach of your sewing machine.

Begin to sew right down the centre of each circle leaving about 10cm of thread at the start of the banner.

Leave about a 3cm gap in between each disc.

When you have run out of discs leave about 10cm of thread on the bottom end.

Hang the banner for a birthday celebration or as a room decoration.

Mr and Mrs Claus

Josephine Helly, Gort Guild, Galway

This jolly pair will be well-loved and admired over Christmas for many years!

You will need

12mm dowelling

200 x 75 x 50mm wood plank

Builder's wire

4 wooden or turned paper beads (for hands)

Stockinette for hands and face

1m bonded interlining

Stuffing (small amount)

50cm polyester wadding

1m marabou or other fluffy material

50cm unbleached calico

2m lace 3½cm deep

Piece of velvet or hessian (Santa's bag)

Gold and red material for dress and cloak (I used curtain material)

Wool (for hair)

Trims of your own choice to decorate

Needle and strong thread

Small piece of round elastic

BASIC FIGURES

For each one, cut a piece of dowelling 30cm long and cut a piece of wood to the following measurements: length 100mm, width 75mm, depth 50mm, to act as the base.

Drill a hole in the centre of each of the pieces of wood of a size that will hold the piece of dowelling firmly in place. Insert the dowelling.

Wrap a strip of interlining around the dowel and stitch in place.

Cut a circle of stockinette approx. 15cm in diameter for the heads.

Run a gathering stitch with strong thread ½cm from the edge and stuff firmly.

When you are satisfied with the shape of your head attach to the top of the dowel and secure firmly in place.

Cut a piece of wire 80cm long, double it and twist it together.

Stitch the centre of the wire to the dowel for the arms approx. 2cm down from the head, and glue a bead on either end for the hands.

With strips of interlining, shape the body starting at the intersection of the dowel (body) and the wire (arms). Criss-cross firmly and stitch to secure with strong thread.

Move out onto the arms and down the body, wrapping and stitching, taking care to build up the arms and body securely.

Wrap a piece of wadding around the body to build it up further and then make a tube of interlining to cover it, securing it with elastic.

Stitch a nice piece of lace around the bottom end to cover the joining of the base to the dowel.

You can cover the base with felt if you wish.

Now you have your basic shape make another the same and have fun dressing them.

MRS CLAUS

Lay the figure down and draw around it to get the pattern for the dress. Measure her shoulder and sleeve and construct the pattern in this way, leaving an opening in the back to put it on.

Leave sleeves a little wide and attach lace trim above the seam turning. Gather around her hands when the dress is on her. Attach marabou to the hem of the dress.

Cut a piece of calico 15 x 30cm for the apron and measure for the band and the straps. Cut these according to the measurements of your figures. Stitch lace in the seams of the straps.

Embroider her eyes, nose and mouth, taking care to achieve the expression you want.

To make the hair, wrap wool around a piece of cardboard 40cm long about 40 times. Remove, cut and stitch down the centre to secure and sew to head. Plait the wool and wrap it around the top of her head.

SANTA CLAUS

Make Santa's undergarment from gold fabric in the same way as Mrs Claus's dress, but without sleeves.

Santa's cloak is measured in the same way but leave 25mm on either side of the front opening for turnings and secure the neck edge with a fastener. Leave sleeves wide and secure with a stitch at his hands. Trim with marabou.

Cut hair for Santa – wrap wool around a piece of cardboard 36cm long about 40 times. Remove, cut and stitch down the centre to secure and sew to the head. For the beard wrap wool around a piece of cardboard 23cm long 20 times and sew to the face. For his moustache wrap wool around card about 20 times, tie in the middle and stitch under the nose.

Now all you have to do is embroider the face, and decorate with his bag of toys and goodies of all sorts.

Two Little Angels

Anne Kavanagh, Annascaul Guild, Kerry

These beautiful Christmas angels look lovely on the mantelpiece during the festive season.

You will need

1 ball no. 10 cotton crochet thread (will make several angels)

2.25mm knitting needles

Styrofoam angels (available in craft store or online)

6 stranded embroidery cotton for hair

Gold or silver paper, or kitchen foil

Laundry starch or hair spray

Tiny beads for halo

Abbreviations

k = knit

p = purl

st(s) = stitch(es)

st st = stocking stitch

tog = together

tbl = through back of loop

yfwd = yarn forward

yrn = yarn round needle

sk2o = slip 1, k2 together, pass slipped stitch over

DRESS

Cast on 95 sts.

1st foundation row: p4, *k1, (p1, k1) 4 times, p4, repeat from * to end.

2nd foundation row: (k2 tog) twice, *p1, (k1, p1) 4 times, (k2 tog) twice, repeat from * to end.

Work in lace pattern as follows:

1st row (right side): p2 *k1, p1, k2 tog tbl, k1, k2 tog, p1, k1, p2, repeat from * to end (65 sts).

2nd row: k2, *p1, k1, p3 tog, k1, p1, k2, repeat from * to end (51 sts).

3rd row: p2, *k1, (yfwd, k1) 4 times, p2, repeat from * to end (79 sts).

4th row: k2, *p1, (k1, p1) 4 times, k2, repeat from * to end.

5th–22nd rows: repeat rows 1–4 4 times, then 1st and 2nd rows again (51 sts).

23rd row: p2 tog, *k1, (yfwd, k1) 4 times, p2 tog, repeat from * to end (71 sts).

24th row: k1, (pl, k1) to end.

25th row: *p1, k1, p1, k2 tog tbl, k1, k2 tog, p1, k1, repeat from * to last st, k1 (43sts).

26th row: *k1, p1, k1, p3 tog, k1, p1, repeat from * to last st, k1 (43 sts).

27th row: *p1, k1, (yfwd, k1) 4 times, repeat from * to last st, p1 (71 sts).

153

28th–34th rows: repeat rows 24–27 once, then rows 24–26 again (43 sts).

35th row: k2 tog, *(yfwd, k1) 3 times, yfwd, sk2o, repeat from * to last 5 sts, (yfwd, k1) 3 times, yfwd, k2 tog (57 sts).

36th row: p1, (k1, p1) to end.

37th row: *k1, p1, k2 tog tbl, k1, k2 tog, p1, repeat from * to last st, k1 (43 sts).

38th row: *p1, k1, p3 tog, k1, repeat from * to last st, p1 (29 sts).

39th row: k1, (yfwd, k1) to end (57 sts).

40th–42nd rows: repeat rows 36–38 (29 sts).

43rd row: *k1, p1, yfwd, k1, yrn, p1, repeat from * to last st, k1 (43 sts).

44th row: p1, (k2, p1) to end.

45th row: (k1, k2 tog tbl, k1, k2 tog) 7 times, k1 (29 sts).

46th row: p1, (p3 tog, p1) to end (15 sts).

47th row: k to end.

48th row: p to end.

49th row: k1, (k2 tog, k2) 3 times, k2 tog (11 sts).

Cast off.

SLEEVES

(makes 1)

Cast on 30 sts.

Work 1st and 2nd foundation rows as for dress (24 sts).

Work lace pattern as follows:

1st–6th rows: work as for dress rows 1–4, then 1st and 2nd row again (16 sts).

7th–10th rows: work as for dress rows 23–26 (13 sts).

11th row: k2 tog, (yfwd, k1) 3 times, yfwd, sk2o, (yfwd, k1) 3 times, yfwd, k2 tog (17sts).

12th–18th rows: work as for dress rows 36–39, then rows 36–38 rows (2 sts).

Cast off.

ARMS

(makes 1)

Cast on 7 sts and, beginning with a knit row, work 18 rows in st st.

Next 2 rows: k4, turn, p4.

Next 2 rows: k3, turn, p3.

Beginning with a knit row, work 18 rows in st st.

Cast off.

LEFT WING

Cast on 26 sts.

1st row (right side): k2 tog, k to end.

2nd row: p18, k to end.

3rd row: k2 tog, k5, (k2 tog) 3 times, (yfwd, k1) 6 times, (k2 tog) 3 times.

4th row: k to end.

Repeat these 4 rows twice more (20 sts).

Next row (picot cast off): cast off 3 sts, *slip st on right-hand needle back on to left-hand needle, cast on 1 st, cast off 3 sts, repeat from * to end.

Cast off.

RIGHT WING

Cast on 26 sts.

1st row (right side): k to last 2 sts, k2 tog.

2nd row: k7, p18.

3rd row: (k2 tog) 3 times, (yfwd, k1) 6 times, (k2 tog) 3 times, k5, k2 tog.

4th row: k to end.

Repeat these 4 rows twice more.

Work picot cast off row and complete as for left wing.

COLLAR

Cast on 8 sts.

1st row (right side): k1, (yfwd, k1) 7 times (15 sts).

2nd row: knit to end

3rd row: k1, (yfwd, k2) 7 times (22 sts).

4th row: knit to end.

Next row (picot cast off): Cast off 2 st, *slip st on right-hand needle back on to left-hand needle, cast on 2 sts, cast off 4 sts, repeat from * to end.

Finish threads.

HEAD AND HAIR

Cut a piece of card 7.5cm wide. Wind approx. 4.5m of embroidery cotton round the card, remove and tie with a single strand at each end of the hank. Back stitch across the middle of the hank securing every strand. Glue hair to the top of the head and draw features on the face.

TO MAKE UP

Sew the centre back seam of the dress. Sew sleeve seams. Thread arms up into the sleeves and secure, giving the appearance of clasped hands. Cover the styrofoam body with gold or silver paper, or use kitchen foil. Place the dress on the body and position the top of the sleeves 6mm from the top edge. Sew the sleeves in place and fasten the neck edge. Join the collar round the neck and tie off. Stiffen the wings with laundry starch or hair spray and sew on. Make a halo from small beads and sew on.

Carrickmacross Lace

Kathleen Kerley, Magheracloone Guild, Monaghan

Carrickmacross Lace was introduced into Ireland in about 1820 by Mrs Grey Porter, the wife of the rector of Donaghmoyne, a small village just outside Carrickmacross, who taught it to local women as a means of supporting their families. Projects such as the ones illustrated are worked in several distinctive stages and each one of them is outlined here.

You will need

Cotton organdie

Fine net (hexagonal mesh)

Design

Pins

White tissue paper

No. 60 crochet cotton in white (known as padding thread)

No. 50 white sewing thread

No. 10 sewing needle

Lace maker's scissors

Tracing paper (to draw or transfer the design)

Waterproof marking pen in black

Use the pen to trace the design on to a piece of tracing paper (traditionally known as butter paper). You can find a selection of general purpose designs on the Internet or in craft books. Place together two layers of tissue paper, your design, a piece of net and then a piece of organdie (in this order, with the organdie on top) and pin at each corner (see figure 1). You now have five layers: organdie, net, pattern, tissue paper x 2. The tissue paper enhances and protects the design while you work on it.

FIGURE 1

Begin by tacking all of these together, starting from the centre and working outwards, ensuring at all times to avoid crossing the design lines on the front of the pattern (see figure 1a).

Repeat this process tacking carefully around the pattern with small tacking stitches including the spaces inside the design where there is no pattern.

FIGURE 1a

FIGURE 1b

Then finally tack the outer edge to prevent the edges curling up as you work (see figure 1b). Do not tack areas of the organdie that will not be cut away as the needle and thread will leave a hole in the organdie when the tacking is removed. Keep all the knots and finished threads to the back, otherwise these will get in the way as you work.

Great care must be taken to keep the threads and organdie clean throughout and to start and finish neatly. Hands should be washed frequently.

Starting from the centre and working from right to left, lay the padding thread exactly on the line of the design holding it down with your left thumb (see figure 2a). Then, using the needle threaded with fine cotton, go through the padding thread, organdie and net for the first stitch (this will secure the thread as there are no knots in Carrickmacross lace)

FIGURE 2a

turning the tail of the sewing thread to the left and sewing over both for 3–4 stitches before cutting the tail of the sewing thread. Do not cut the padding thread – leave it attached to the ball. Then continue to sew around the design, just picking up the organdie and net but not the design or the tissue paper, until the end is reached. Finish off by doing an anchor stitch (buttonhole stitch) before you cut the padding thread. The padding thread must always be cut first, then using the sewing thread do two more anchor stitches to secure the end before cutting the sewing thread. Remember that the stitches should be close enough and tight enough to hold the padding thread, organdie and net firmly together after the design is cut out.

GUIPURE

This is a process where portions of the net and organdie are entirely cut away and bars are inserted. The execution of this technique is worked at the same time as the couching of the pattern. An example of this can be seen on the dove's wing. This is done by attaching three strands of sewing thread from the centre of the wing to the edge to make a padding thread before sewing over all three with a buttonhole stitch.

LOOPS

The next step is to begin the picot or loop edge (see figure 2b). Attach the padding thread to the organdie and net as previously described, around the outer edge of the design. Twist the padding thread in a clockwise direction to form a loop and while holding it down with your thumb put three couching stitches inside to hold the loop in place. Then pull the padding thread to adjust the loop to the required size. Next, outside the loop put in two couching stitches.

Repeat this process all the way around the border.

FIGURE 2b

CUTTING OUT

When the loops have been completed, the tacking stitches are removed along with the pattern from the back of the work (see figure 3). Separate the organdie and net and slit the organdie with a pair of lace scissors. Insert the rounded end of the lace scissors between the organdie and net layers and very carefully cut away the surplus organdie around the design.

FILLING STITCHES

Filling or embroidery stitches worked on the net are an individual choice as each lace maker has a collection of decorative stitches through which they can achieve a wide variety of effects. A selection of these can be found in lace books and the ICA runs classes dealing with this specifically.

FIGURE 3

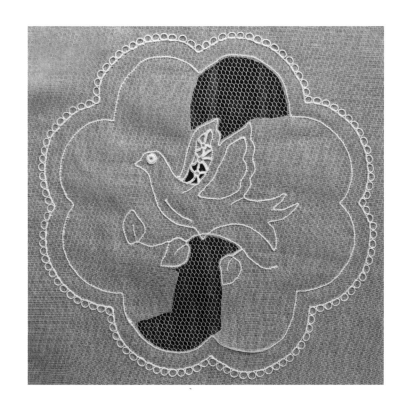

FIGURE 4

POPS

These are small decorative circles made using the No. 50 thread and are the last part of the design to be worked. These are sewn only after the organdie has been cut away, as they are worked on the net (see figure 4). Outline or trace around one of the holes in the net with the sewing thread to form a tiny circle. Then using a buttonhole stitch catch in this thread, securing the loose end of the tracing thread as the pop is worked. Push the needle through eye first so as not to damage the threads. Continue buttonholing until a neatly formed pop has been made.

Mini Wreath

Mary O'Gorman, Maynooth Guild, Kildare

These mini wreaths can be hung on the Christmas tree or around the house for a festive feel.

You will need

3 different 'fat quarters' (46 x 56cm pieces) of Christmas fabric

½m 70gsm wadding

Gold crochet thread (optional)

Sewing thread

Coordinating ribbon

Sewing needle, pins and safety pin

Trinkets to decorate (optional, e.g. from a Christmas cracker)

Cotton tape

Cut 3 strips of 30 x 6cm of fabric (1 from each fabric). Cut 3 strips of wadding 30 x 5cm.

Cut a 60cm piece of gold thread (if using). Cut 3 x 38cm strips of cotton tape.

Fold the fabric strips in half lengthways, right side in, inserting the cotton tape by the fold, and pin at the top. Lay 1 of the folded strips over the wadding with the folded edge of the material to the centre of the wadding.

Pin in place and stitch across the top, securing the end of the cotton tape, and down by the raw edges along the centre of the wadding.

To turn, fold the wadding over, gently pull the tape and ease the material in at the top; keep pulling gently until the strip is turned right side out. Do the same with the other 2 strips.

Cut the tape off as near to the edge as possible, taking care not to cut the material. Fold the gold thread (if using) in half and stitch to 1 of the strips.

Place the 3 pieces over each other slightly staggered, with the gold thread strip in the middle, and top sew together.

Start plaiting, keeping the gold thread in place as you work down the plait.

As you near the end use a safety pin to hold the plait in place.

Turn in the ends of each strip with a seam, catching the gold thread in as you close the middle one. Finish off the plait and top stitch the 3 pieces together.

Bring the 2 ends of the plait together using a ladder stitch, by picking a stitch from alternate pieces, pulling up tightly as you go, turning the wreath as you go to stitch the other side; do this a couple of times to secure your wreath.

Flatten the wreath and, with the side with the gold thread facing you, stitch a trinket over the seam. Cut a piece of ribbon about 18cm long to hang the wreath. Fold it in half and stitch over the seam. Cut another piece of ribbon and make a bow to stitch over the hanging ribbon.

Christmas Table Runner and Place Mats

Mary O'Gorman, Maynooth Guild, Kildare

These very straightforward projects will add a lovely festive touch to your table at Christmas time.

You will need

1m Christmas fabric

¼m or 'fat quarter' of contrasting Christmas fabric

1m calico (unbleached or bleached)

1m plain fabric for base of mats and runner

1m batting

½m Bondaweb

Templates
(you can make these yourself by drawing simple Christmassy shapes onto stiff card, or for a real shortcut you can buy festive fabric that comes with the shape preprinted on it)

Cardboard and pencil

Sewing thread

Sewing needles and pins

Sewing machine (optional)

Cut 6 pieces of calico 33 x 25cm for the place mats and 3 pieces 21 x 21cm for the table runner.

Trace designs onto cardboard and cut out the templates. Trace around the templates to mark the design on the main Christmas material and cut out.

Iron the pieces of Christmas material onto the Bondaweb, right side facing you. (To protect the iron I use a piece of greaseproof paper over the material.)

Peel the material from the Bondaweb backing and iron the pieces onto the calico (again using greaseproof paper to protect the iron).

Stitch around the designs using whatever stitch you like, e.g. back stitch, buttonhole, blanket stitch, or machine using zigzag or straight stitch.

For the runner, from the contrasting material cut 4 pieces 21 x 9cm and 2 pieces 90 x 9cm.

Stitch the 4 shorter pieces of material to either side of the 3 smaller calico squares to make a long strip, open seams and press flat.

Sew the 2 longer pieces of material to each side of this long strip and press the seams flat.

From the batting cut 1 piece 90 x 38cm for the runner and cut 6 pieces 33 x 25cm for the place mats. Cut pieces the same size from the plain fabric.

To assemble the place mats and runner, place the plain material on a flat surface, then the batting and then the top piece with the design on it and pin in place.

Cut 6.5cm strips across the width of the main Christmas fabric to bind the mats and runner. You will need at least 9 strips, maybe more, depending on the width of the fabric.

Join 3 strips at the short ends, press seams flat and fold the strips in half wrong sides together and press. Fold and press the other strips also.

To attach to runner and mats, place raw edges together with right sides facing. Pin and stitch in place making sure to allow sufficient material to turn the corner. Fold over the material and slip stitch in place on the underside.

Hat Pin Cushion

Mary O'Gorman, Maynooth Guild, Kildare

These pin cushions are made with Christmas fabric for a seasonal gift, but of course you could use any fabric you like to make them.

You will need

'Fat quarter' piece or ½m material

1m lace

Card (cereal box)

Pencil

Toy stuffing

Ribbon to hang

Sewing thread

Sewing needles

Cut an 18cm circle of fabric for the base and cut a 14cm circle of fabric for the top.

Cut a 10cm circle of card for the base.

Cut a piece of lace approximately 40cm long and a piece of ribbon approximately 15cm for hanging.

Using double thread run a gathering stitch around the large circle of fabric and place the card in the middle. Pull it up tight around it and fasten off.

Using double thread, gather the small circle in the same way and stuff the centre with a little toy stuffing, pull up tight and fasten off.

Attach the top to the base by stitching round, picking up a piece of material alternating top and bottom each time, until it is tightly secured. Fasten off.

Run a row of gathering stitches round the top of the lace and fit round the middle of the hat, pull up tight and fasten off.

Fold the piece of ribbon in half and stitch to the back of the hat to hang it by.

DIY Ribbon Dispenser

You will need

Old pasta sauce jar

Paint/spray paint

Ribbon

Knife/drill

Clean out your empty sauce jar and dry thoroughly.

Using a sharp knife make a hole in the lid of your jar big enough to fit your ribbon through, or you can use a drill if you prefer.

Paint the jar and lid in the colour of your choice and leave to dry.

Once dry paint another layer and leave to dry again.

Once it is completely dry put the ribbon inside your jar and pull the ribbon through the hole at the top.

Christmas Card Holder

Pat O'Looney, Botanic Glasnevin Guild, Dublin

This is a great way to display your Christmas cards, year after year. The finished size of the holder will be approximately 23 x 107cm.

You will need

46 x 115cm piece of Christmas craft fabric

46 x 115cm piece of calico or other cream fabric for pockets and pocket backing

23 x 115cm piece of bonded curtain lining (you can substitute batting and curtain lining instead)

1 small ring to hang holder

Gold tassel or ornament of your choice to hang from the bottom of the holder

Sewing machine or needle and thread

Cut 4 23cm squares from Christmas fabric and 4 23cm squares from calico or cream fabric.

Mark a diagonal line on the wrong side of the fabric on each of the 4 cream squares and then mark a line ½cm each side of the diagonal (see figure 1).

Place a cream square and a Christmas fabric square right sides together and stitch along the lines marked each side of the diagonal – you can do this by hand or machine. Cut along the diagonal line. This gives you 2 pockets comprising a triangle of cream and a triangle of Christmas print. Turn right side out and press lightly. Do this with all 4 squares of Christmas and cream material, giving you 8 pockets in total.

Cut a strip 23cm wide across the full width of the cream fabric (115cm). Fold this in half lengthwise and mark the centre line by tacking down the fold.

To make the triangular shape at the top and bottom of the holder take each corner of the backing and fold it in to meet at the line, then press and trim off these triangular pieces. Then mark a line 18½cm from the bottom point and cut off this piece and put aside carefully (see figure 2). The last pocket should be sandwiched between this piece and the backing. Accurate measurement is important to the finished appearance of the holder.

Begin constructing your holder by pinning the first pocket along its lower edge as shown in figure 3. Then, alternating sides, place remaining pockets with about 8½cm between them (this may have to be adjusted slightly). The pockets overlap each other. It is important the pockets are aligned with the backing. They are turned down, stitched in place and then flipped back up. The last pocket should be stitched into the seam joining the backing piece and the piece cut off the backing (see figure 4).

When all the pockets are stitched in place at the base, flip them up and tack all around the edge of the holder, catching the sides of the pockets in place. Now attach the holder to the bonded lining with another row of tacking and trim lining to the edge of the holder.

Cut enough 2½cm-wide bias strips from the remainder of the Christmas fabric to fit all around the edge of the holder, fold in half lengthways and press lightly. With right sides together place along the edge of the hanging and sew ½cm in from the edge all round the hanging, fold over, then slip stitch all around the back.

Attach the ring to the top for hanging. You may need to reinforce the top piece to keep it from sagging when the cards are placed in it. (To do this make a small pocket at the back across the base of the top triangle for a piece of a wooden skewer or of a wire coat hanger cut to size.) Attach the tassel to the bottom and put a decoration of your choice on the top and bottom of the holder.

Next roll back the edge of the pockets and press lightly. Then put in a small stitch to keep the roll in place.

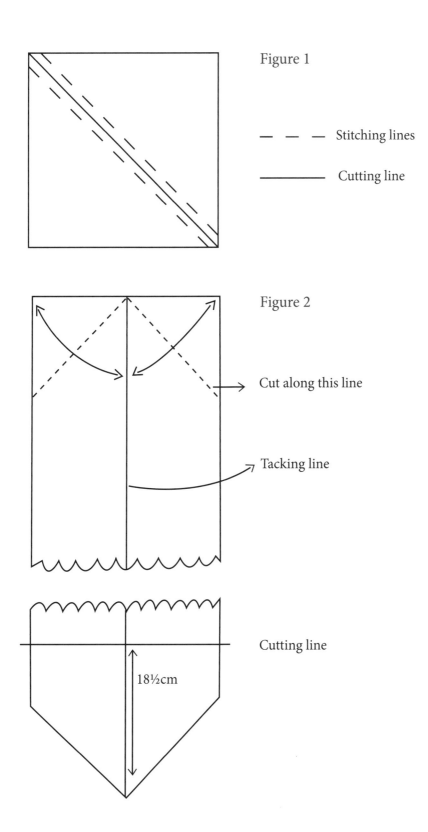

Figure 1

− − − Stitching lines

——— Cutting line

Figure 2

Cut along this line

Tacking line

Cutting line

18½cm

183

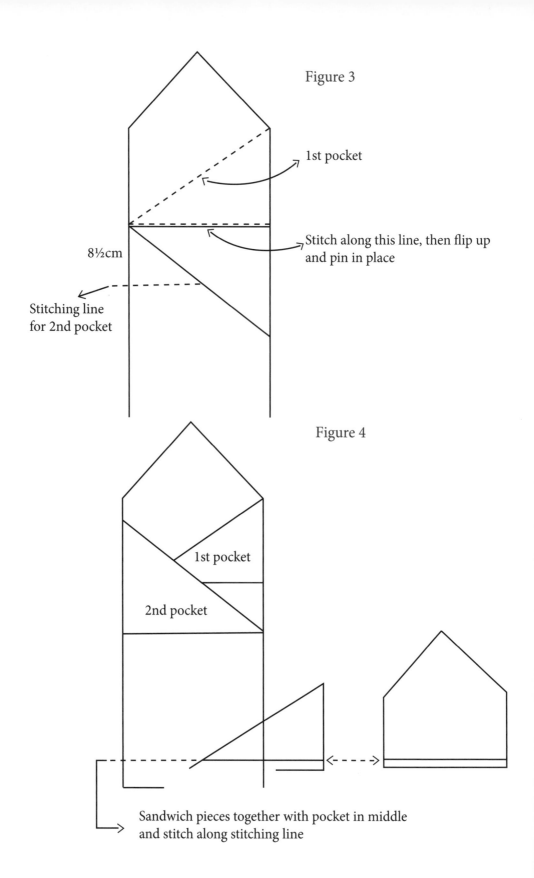

Figure 3

1st pocket

Stitch along this line, then flip up
and pin in place

8½cm

Stitching line
for 2nd pocket

Figure 4

1st pocket

2nd pocket

Sandwich pieces together with pocket in middle
and stitch along stitching line

Knitted Easter Chick

Margaret Horan, Clonmel Guild, Tipperary South

These cute little chicks can be used as egg warmers or to hide chocolate eggs at Easter.

You will need

Double knitting wool

3.25mm knitting needles

Small piece of orange felt

Small piece of ribbon

Darning needle

Sewing needle and thread

Cast on 26 stitches.

Knit 2 rows in garter (plain) stitch.

Increase 1 stitch at the beginning of each of the next 12 rows (38 stitches).

Cast off 9 stitches at the beginning of the next 2 rows (20 stitches). Knit 8 rows.

Cut the wool leaving a 40cm length.

Thread the end of the wool through a darning needle.

Bring the needle through the stitches, removing them from the knitting needle at the same time.

Pull the wool tightly to draw the stitches together and sew the sides of the chick together, leaving the bottom open.

Using black or dark wool sew an eye on either side of the head. Stuff the head with cotton wool (optional).

Cut a small diamond-shaped piece from the felt and sew it onto the chick as a beak.

Finish by tying the ribbon around the chick's neck and add a few stitches to hold it in place.

Homemade Blackboard Sign

You will need

30 x 20cm piece of marine plywood

Blackboard paint

White water-based matt paint for frame

Paintbrush

2½ x ½cm beading – 2 lengths 30cm long and 2 lengths 15cm long

Wood glue

Cord for hanging

Paint the piece of marine plywood with blackboard paint and leave to dry.

Paint the beading with white paint, or any colour you wish, and leave to dry.

Glue 30cm beading to the front of the plywood, top and bottom, flush to edge; leave to dry.

Glue 15cm beading to the front at the sides, flush to edge; leave to dry.

Drill 2 holes through the side of the beading that you want to be at the top.

Put the ends of the cord through the 2 holes and knot so that it is secure.

CONTRIBUTORS

Anne Kavanagh, Annascaul Guild, Kerry

Anne Payne, Portlaoise Guild, Laois

Anne Maria Dennison, Mainistir Na Féile Guild, Limerick

Betty Gorman, Castletown Guild, Laois

Betty Teahan, Wicklow Town Guild, Wicklow

Breda Baker, Annascaul Guild, Kerry

Brenda Leary, Blackrock Guild, Louth

Bridgid Keane, Ardmore Grange Guild, Waterford

Carol Lynch, Muff Guild, Donegal

Elaine Hynes, Castlebar Guild, Mayo

Helen O'Sullivan, Derryquay Guild, Kerry

Helen Weir, Two-Mile-House Guild, Kildare

Josephine Helly, Gort Guild, Galway

Kathleen Kerley, Magheracloone Guild, Monaghan

Kay Murray, Broadford Guild, Clare

Mairead Cullen O'Gorman, Camross Guild, Wexford

Margaret Clince, Garristown Guild, Dublin

Margaret Horan, Clonmel Guild, Tipperary South

Mary O'Gorman, Maynooth Guild, Kildare

Maura Davis, Delgany Guild, Wicklow

Maura Riordan, Dun Laoghaire Guild, Dublin

Maureen Neary, Brickens Guild, Mayo

Nora Keady, Moycullen Guild, Galway

Pat O'Looney, Botanic Glasnevin Guild, Dublin

Pauline O'Dwyer, Marlay Guild, Dublin

Réiltín MacCana, Dun Laoghaire Guild, Dublin

Rose Harris (RIP), Sevenhouses Guild, Kilkenny

Statia Ivers, Ballycoog Guild, Wicklow

Wanda McCamley, Delgany Guild, Wicklow

CREDITS

Photography by Joanne Murphy

Styling by Orla Neligan

Assistants to photographer and stylist: Liosa MacNamara and Ali Coughlan

Model: Mary MacNamara

THANKS TO:

Take Me Home Ltd: Unit 20 Nutgrove Shopping Centre, Rathfarnham, Dublin 14. Specialising in wool, haberdashery, occasional furniture, giftware and kitchen accessories. **W:** www.takemehome.ie

Avoca: HQ Kilmacanogue, Bray, Co. Wicklow. **T:** (01) 2746939; **W:** www.avoca.ie; **E:** info@avoca.ie

Meadows & Byrne: Dublin, Cork, Galway, Clare, Tipperary. **T:** (01) 2804554/(021) 4344100; **W:** www.meadowsandbyrne.com; **E:** info@meadowsandbyrne.ie

Harold's Bazaar: 208 Harold's Cross Road, Dublin 6W. **T:** 086 7228789

Harryali: T: 087 7758547; **W:** www.harryali.ie; **E:** hello@harryali.ie

Historic Interiors: Oberstown, Lusk, Co. Dublin. **T:** 01 8437174; **E:** killian@historicinteriors.net

A. Rubanesque Ltd: Powerscourt Townhouse Centre, 59 South William St, Dublin 2. **T:** (01) 672 9243; **W:** arubanesque.ie; **E:** ribbons@arubanesque.ie

Liz Wall would like to acknowledge two books she used when researching her introduction: G. Mitchell, *Deeds not Words: the life and work of Muriel Gahan* (Dublin, 1997) and A. Heverin, *The Irish Countrywomen's Association: a history, 1910–2000* (Dublin, 2000).